BACK TO THE EAST

INDIA, KASHMIR AND NEPAL

by

ALUN BUFFRY

Back to the East
India, Kashmir and Nepal
by
Alun Buffry
Published by ABeFree Publishing, 2021

ISBN 978-1-9163107-9-7

Appreciation

Thanks to the Baktoo family in Srinagar.
Thanks to Simon King and Steve Land for proof reading.
Thanks to ABeFree Publishing for formatting the soft-back edition.
http://www.buffry.org.uk/abefreepublishing.html

ABOUT THE AUTHOR

Alun Buffry was born in South Wales in 1950 and lived there until 1968 when he moved to Norwich to study chemistry at the University of East Anglia. He graduated in 1971.

After leaving University, he travelled overland to India on what became known as The Hippy Trail, with little money or guidance and where he became ill. After he returned to Norwich, he became a follower of Prem Rawat, known in those days as Guru Maharaji and he remains a follower this day.

BY THE SAME AUTHOR

	ISBN
From Dot to Cleopatra: History of Ancient Egypt	978-1-8872910-9-8
All About My Hat: The Hippy Trail 1972	978-0-9932107-0-9
Time for Cannabis: The Prison Years 1991 to 1995	978-0-9932107-6-1
Damage and Humanity in Custody	978-1-5330262-2-4
Out of Joint: 20 Years of Campaigning for Cannabis	978-1-5084202-1-7
Myhat in Egypt: Through the Eyes of A God	978-0-9932107-7-8
The Effie Enigma; The Motherless Mothers	978-0-9932107-9-2
Inside My Hat and Other Heads	978-1-9163107-0-4
Words of Weed and Wisdom	978-1-9163107-6-6
If Only Suomi	978-1-9163107-7-3
Legalise and Utilise Commemorative	979-8-7048950-4-6

CONTENTS

INTRODUCTION

I had not been to India since 1972, a strange trip with no previous foreign travel experience, very little money and not a lot of common sense. So after several months of travelling overland by various means of transport, including coaches, cars, trucks, on the back of a motorbike, a horse and cart, a tractor, a train and even a boat, we had reached Lahore in Pakistan and took a plane to the land of rickshaws. A few weeks there and I became sick. I spent time in hospital in Delhi, Kabul and Tehran, eventually flying back to the UK from there. But I survived. Not everyone did in those days. But it was an unforgettable experience that cannot be repeated today. That story is told in my book which is also on Amazon and Kindle: 'All About My Hat The Hippy Trail 1972'.

I had wanted to go back the India, such a mixture of good and bad places and experiences, ever since.

My next trip there was to be a holiday on the houseboats of Kashmir, with a pony trek along the way, with a friend called Lizzy, in 1981.

In 1985 I made a two month journey around Northern India, Nepal and Kashmir with Lesley.

This book was written up from my notebooks from those times. I have included some scanned photos and poems.

Many of the descriptions of places, temples and such, have been copied from entries in my journals of the times which themselves were copied from pamphlets. However, I have also added in more up-to-date information from on-line, to make them more complete.

1981 Kashmir with Lizzy.

5th October: Delhi

We left Heathrow on Kuwait Airways flight KU380 22.00, Boing 747. The flight was great with some excellent views over the Alps and later of the coastlines of Yugoslavia (as it was then) and Greece. We arrived at Kuwait airport in darkness. It was noticeably new and clean; we did not have a long wait before we were on the 747 again, to Delhi.

We took a dusty taxi ride to the Hotel Asia where we had a double room booked. Apparently, we were told, all the taxi fares had gone up 50%, presumably specially for us.

The smell of Delhi was so familiar to me; it hadn't changed in 9 years. It was already very hot and dusty so the first thing was a few hours rest before we go to the Air India office.

After going to the office and confirming our stay on a houseboat in Kashmir, we went to a good looking and clean looking restaurant near Connaught Circus for dinner.

The food was actually quite good, the service friendly and the décor pleasant.

Yet after we had finished, I saw a look of horror on Lizzy's face, as she sat opposite me. She pointed at the window. I turned to see a rat on the window sill. I called the waiter. He calmly walked towards it shaking a tea towel. The rat ran out of the open window.

We slept well, however, that night. I did not dream of rats!

6th October

We spent the day riding round Old Delhi and New Delhi on a tuk-tuk, a three wheeler scooter.

Our first stop was the Lal Qila or Red Fort, with its huge gardens and many red stone buildings which were constructed in 1639 by the fifth Mughal Emperor Shah Jahan (of Taj Mahal fame) as the palace of his fortified capital Shahjahanabad when he decided to move his capital from Agra to Delhi. Lai means red and Quila means fortress.

The Red Fort is named after its massive enclosing walls of red sandstone. The imperial apartments consist of a row of pavilions, connected by a water channel known as the Stream of Paradise. Many of the buildings are now used by Government administration.

We spent the afternoon trying to get flights for tomorrow to Srinagar, but they are all booked, so we went to the train station instead. After queueing some time, an Indian lady approached us and said we did not have to queue, as ladies could just go straight to the front. So we went to the front and Lizzy bought first class tickets one way, which cost 400 rupees, about £25.

Fortunately the room was air conditioned as my head was spinning from all the politeness, ramblings and bargaining.

It's strange, as I always think of India as being Holy, slow and dreamy, whereas Delhi was fast and dusty and the main religion seems to be money, everybody wanting it but few having it. There are a lot of luxury hotels and offices and guys dressed in suits but far more poor people and beggars in rags. The roads are crowded with buses, trucks, cars, motorised tuk-tuks, bicycles and bicycle rickshaws, donkey carts and even an elephant. People drive on their horns. The rule on the road was Might Is Right.

8th October: Srinagar

It was Thursday. A lot seemed to have happened since Tuesday. It was a long train ride. Yesterday, we caught the 16.00 train from Delhi to Jammu. The first class compartment with two tier sleepers was not even up to third class in the UK but we did get tea and a meal and at least we could stretch out, if not sleep. We met an Indian family that had lived in Zambia but moved to London.

We arrived in Jammu about 8 AM (two hours late) and met up with Mary, an English girl who was planning to marry Ahmed Baktoo, the son of a houseboat owner. Also there was Abdullah, a Kashmiri chap, who worked at the Himalayan Holidays company offices. We took a taxi with them to Srinagar, which took nine hours, stopping for tea and meals.

Mary was a very pleasant, red-haired young lady who seemed to be very much in love with India, especially Kashmir although she did not tell us much about here previous experiences.

On the road we saw where rockfalls and landslides had partially blocked the road and disrupted the heavy flow of trucks and buses. It seemed too remote for rapid repairs; remembering this was India, it could take years. We passed many hundreds of people, some driving goats or sheep, and some camels and some monkeys watching to see what they could grab.

The road passes through, or rather up and down, two valleys in Jammu, before entering the Kashmir Valley. The views, as much as we could see out of the taxi windows, were incredible. There was no stopping for photos but I did get one or two.

There were road signs reading 'Better Late Than Never', 'Avoid a Crash and Don't be Rash' and 'No Hurry, No Worry'.

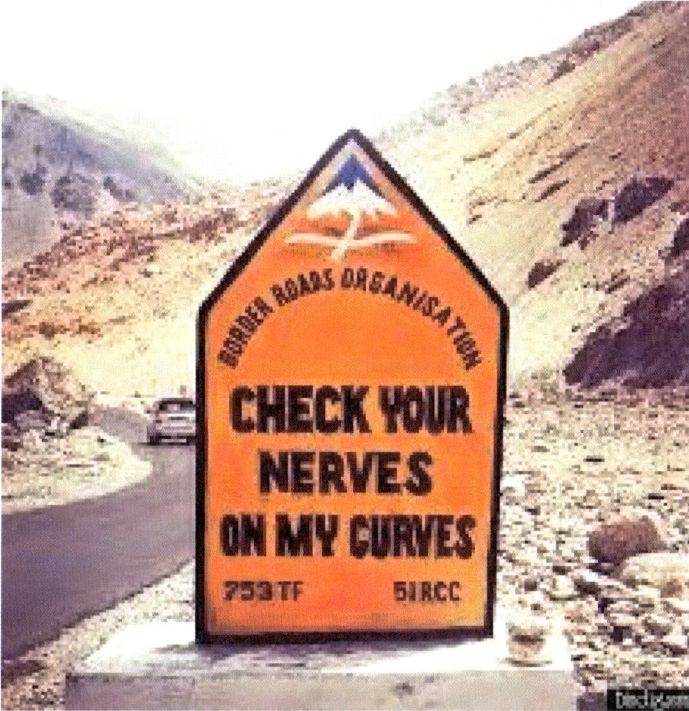

Not
that it deterred all drivers – we saw three overturned trucks.

'Keep Your Nerves on the Curves!', 'Alcohol in for Refreshment, not for Intoxication', 'Life is short, Don't Make it Shorter'.

Other signs read 'Spray your house with DDT' and 'This is not a Rally, Drive Slow in Kashmir Valley'.

Also a sign suggesting a stop for one's first view of the Kashmir Valley.

I have forgotten so much I was going to write about. Lizzy asking "Why have those men driven their trucks into the river?" Me: "You can drive a truck to the river but you can't make it drink."

The road there included a tunnel built by Germany in 1958 and over 1.5 miles long, guarded at each end, with photography prohibited. One way was closed that day, so we had to wait for traffic coming towards us to clear. The other tunnel was full of donkeys and goats. After a section of treacherous road, it descends into the valley. Beautiful! Then what was after quite a long way, but suddenly, we arrived in Srinagar.

Srinagar

Upon safe arrival in Srinagar, we transferred by shikara boat to the beautiful Kashmir Paradise houseboat. All meals provided, and now, need a rest.

Srinagar was the largest city and the summer capital of the Indian union territory of Jammu and Kashmir. It lies on the banks of the Jhelum river, which was called Vyath in Kashmir, a tributary of the Indus and on the Dal, Nageen and Anchar lakes. The river passes through the city and meanders through the valley, moving onward and deepening in the Wular Lake. The city was known for its nine old bridges, connecting the two parts of the city. The city was also known for its natural environment, its gardens, waterfronts and houseboats. It was also known for traditional Kashmiri handicrafts, walnut carvings, carpets, shawls and dried fruits. Srinagar was often called The Venice of the East.

On the houseboat we met an English guy, John, who works on the Daily Mail and an American couple who work in Saudi Arabia, but they are leaving tomorrow.

The other guy that we met and became fond of was Habib. He was not one of the Baktoo brothers but brought us our meals, cleaned up and looked after us well. They called him "the servant" but I did not like to call him that.

The dinner was good, the evening was cool and I look forward to seeing our surroundings in daylight the next day.

Not being able to swim and not being over keen on boats, I must say that I found this houseboat safe and forgot that we were actually afloat all the time.

HABIB

9th October.

I slept for eleven hours. Much needed.

Toast and marmalade for breakfast. The room was quite luxurious especially by Indian standards, with wooden walls and carpets on the floor. The mesh at the windows and the wooden ceiling was decorated with interlocking twelve-sided shapes.

Apparently, like most things I guess, the weather in India had been strange for the last few years; the summers were getting longer and this year there was no monsoon in the North.

We went for a ride to see the Perfume Garden houseboat, the pride and joy of the Baktoos and to meet the head of the family, Mr Baktoo, whom Mary said was a devoted Moslem who had been to Mecca.

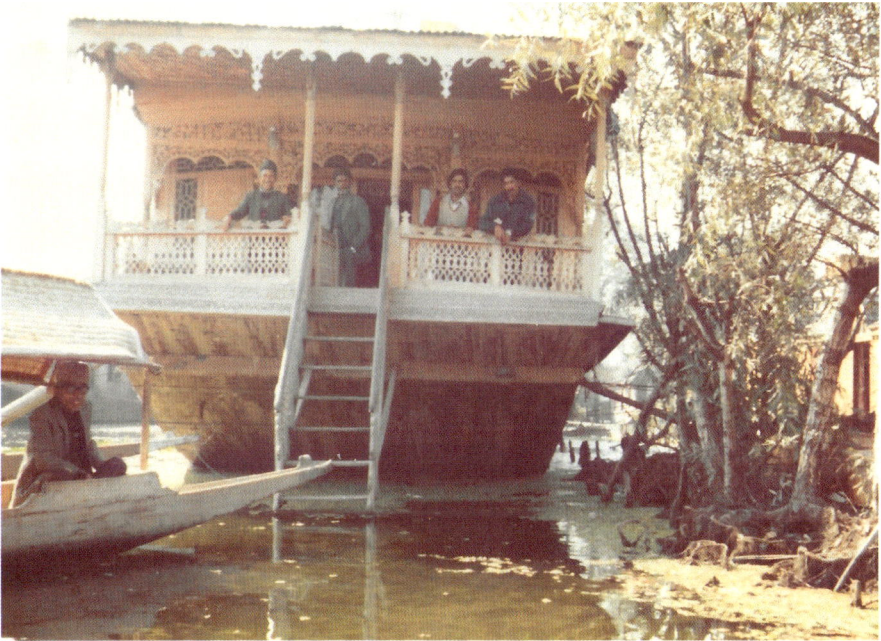

The journey by shikara took an hour each way; it was superb, slow and peaceful and relaxing, surrounded by still unspoilt beauty. The water in lake Nageen was so still, the reflections of the mountains and houseboats doubling the beauty. They allowed swimming and had water-skiing there.

There were all sorts of houseboats, large deluxe for rental and smaller ones that people live in. By the side of the lake were hotels, shops and stalls, with the beautiful mountains behind them. A treasure to hold in the heart.

Apparently some of the buildings on the lakeside were three hundred years old.

Sharing a Shikara ride with Mary

When the British were here, the local Government was able to ban foreigners from buying land. Nowadays, the large houseboats cost tens and even hundreds of thousands of pounds, so many local businessmen had made partnerships with foreign investors. Kashmir Paradise, for instance, was part owned by Mr Baktoo and part owned by a German. Mr Baktoo had several sons, Ali, Farook, and Jimmy (Mohammed); there was no mention of daughters. The father talked to us about the possibility of us selling Kashmir holidays back in the UK. I told him about the Norfolk Broads,

The return journey was just as good but it was getting cool. We

11

passed several groups of children singing their equivalent of Christmas carols and there were firecrackers and rockets.

There were lotus plants and reeds on the lake and lots of ducks and other birds.

I took a photo of the shikara man (above) and promised to send him a print.

The dinner that evening was excellent, vegetarian for me and lamb for Lizzy and Mary, but they both wanted to eat some of mine: curry vegetables, spinach aloo, spicy cabbage, pilau rice, chapati, bean bhaji, apple stew, apple juice and chai.

Lizzy was a small and thin English girl from Sheffield, slightly younger than me. She could be short-tempered and sharp-spoken, but generally meant well. She was very much an environmentalist. I had know her for about ten years before this journey.

10th October

We took a shikara to the landing spot and waked into town. We went to the Post Office and also to pre-book our tickets back to Delhi for the 23rd. Lizzy went off to buy a swimming costume.

The town itself was like most towns, full of people, hustle and bustle, yet somehow still slow. At one point Lizzy ran across the road to buy tobacco. As I watched I saw almost everyone else stop to watch her! People did not run in the streets of Srinagar unless it was an emergency!

Many of the shops were selling paper maché boxes, carpets and such, for tourists, but there were few beggars and those that were there had apparently come from Delhi, so we were told.

I wondered whether the Kashmir craftsmen would make Welsh dressers.

There are seventeen languages in India. Religions include Islam, Hinduism, Christianity, Buddhism, Sikhism, Jainism, Judaism. In Kashmir they are mostly Islam. Pakistan wanted Kashmir, coincidentally India's richest state. Personally I hoped it either became independent or stays in India, as I think Pakistan would industrialise it too much.

Unlike much of India, there was a lot of meat eaten there in Kashmir but not pig, although vegetarian food was also easy to get. Three of the four sheep that were outside the houseboat on a clump of grass had disappeared. We were told that they had been slaughtered, one for the family, one for the relations and friends and one for the poor.

Some had appeared on our dinner table for Lizzy and Mary. Lizzy would not eat it even though she normally ate meat.

11th October

Awoke for a hot shower and breakfast of porridge, fried eggs, toast and tea. I bought some nice papier-maché boxes and egg cups; good quality.

The Charas here was quite strong. Just a one-skinner (tobacco joint) was enough to share. We could not finish a three-skinner between us that evening.

Kashmir green tea was delicious. It made a change from sweet milky chai.

The Sikh couple, Ravi and Rami, that were staying here had gone to stay in a hut in Gulmarg to do some walking. They were planning to stay on the houseboat for a few days and they suggested we go to visit them. Of course, if we had, they may have been out walking. Ravi was a captain in the Indian army and also a part-time farmer. His father was a judge in Delhi, he said

The afternoon was spent on a shikara ride to Lake Nageen to the other houseboat and Lizzy took a swim. I thought that I would not be surprised if she became ill later. We passed the floating gardens on the way, where they grow vegetables during the summer.

Again it was quiet and dreamy on the lake and on the houseboat with the occasional smoke.

12th October

We went to see the Forewest Wood Emporium

The quality of the craftsmanship was excellent and impressive. I thought that I could sell some back in the UK. Statues, Buddhas, tables and chairs, boxes and lamp stands, chests and nests of tables, a writing bureau, chess tables, sewing boxes and wine cabinets.

We crossed the Golden Lake where houseboats were joined together for large groups of guests. Sometimes there were just planks of wood between them, so guests literally had to walk the plank.

I spent the afternoon sitting on the sun deck relaxing and smoking, Lizzy was sick.

She would not accept that it was connected to her having swam in the lake. She was fasting for the day. Mary also had diarrhoea, so maybe it was the meat. Apparently she had suffered with jaundice and typhoid in Delhi a few weeks previously.

13th October

I was almost forgetting which day of the week it was, not that it mattered. We went back to the town and I bought a Kashmir sweater for about £5.

Cashing a travellers cheque took ten minutes as people pass around their forms while we waited. Then off to the post office to get letters and postcards franked so nobody can steam off the stamps, which was apparently common in India.

The previous night, Mr Baktoo had spent an hour telling Lizzy that in India she could become a guru! I couldn't imagine why he would think that. He had said that he had been to Mecca. In his younger days, he said, he used to drink alcohol and smoke, but stopped. In fact he still smoked joints. He smoked joints with us, as did his sons, but as soon as one of the others appeared, they put down the joint. They each asked us not to tell the others. Yussef did not smoke. He secretly drank whiskey though. By the time Mr Baktoo stopped talking, Lizzy was very stoned, so she went to crash out.

Mr Baktoo

We stayed on the Kashmir Paradise that night.

At 8.30 PM was the only one still up.

The room was lovely, with its own bathroom and WC, but the

massive double bed was not at all comfortable. Once the light was turned off it was pitch dark.

KASHMIR LAKES

by

Alun Buffry

Mogul sounds, ring round

The glorious snow-capped mounds.

Sheep and cows, outside now,

The friendly servant humbly bows.

The air is cold, the valley bold,

The view, the peace the beauty sold,

For rupees, pounds or marks,

Or items brought from Marks and Sparks.

The atmosphere here is safe for sure.

The beggars try to ask for more.

The market places always full,

Of paper maché, carpets of wool.

The walnut carvings are the best,

In all the world, east or west!

The peace that finds itself so near,

Is peace that travels everywhere.

14th October

We went to a carpet factory with Mr Baktoo; also it's a sales room, of course. The carpets, silk and wool in various size, were beautiful. I bought a woollen one, five by three feet, for £220, probably paying too much, but I was stoned. It had 440 knots per square metre and supposed to be top quality. I paid just 200 rupees deposit and had to send the rest from the UK.

The following day, we had planned to go for three days camping and pony trekking.

We knew little about where we are going or how hard the walking will be, but we are assured that everything will be provided and Mary, Ahmed's wife-to-be, was coming along with us.

We were told it will be just six miles moving each day over three hours.

The French couple that had been staying here warned us about cobras; they said that the army tents that they had seen all had anti-cobra precautions. Mr Baktoo said there are no cobras in the mountains.

Lizzy bought a sweater and some plimsolls for walking, but I thought they would not much good, she needed good boots. I told her but she would not listen.

Whilst we were strolling around, we passed a park. I spotted some weed growing near the wall, so pulled off some heads and dried it in the sun back on the deck of the houseboat. It was a nice smoke.

Apparently, as we were told, the family was a strong unit here and when a man took a wife she lived with her parents and did not see much of her own family. Divorces were rare and considered shameful, so much so that the wives of the brothers of the divorcees brothers may even divorce their own husbands. Men were the bosses of the families. Mr Baktoo said women should serve; not Lizzy apparently as he had said she should be a guru!

15th October: Pahalgam

We left Srinagar to Pahalgam by taxi. We passed a wedding precession on the way.

The groom was being carried and covered with money and flowers and surrounded by people. We didn't see the bride. She was probably washing dishes already.

The taxi journey took a few hours. We stopped on the way so they could buy some chicken.

By the time we arrived, our tents were pitched in the 'Familiarisation Camp'. We were set behind a half-dried up

river, called Aru, I thought, with three tents and some donkeys. All the equipment was here, for cooking etc and so were our cook and guide.

It turned out the chickens were alive and one had disappeared already. Lizzy seemed very philosophical, asking questions such as "Why does God allow suffering? Why did he create evil?"

Then Lizzy and Mary went off for a short pony ride whilst I stayed and contemplated the river; but wherever I sat, on the cushions, there seemed to already be a chicken hiding there. Silly things, if they had known their destiny they would have run off, but no, they just hung about the camp.

River Alive!
by Alun Buffry

Whether we laugh, or whether we cry,
The river of life goes rushing by,
Down the hills and mountain sides,
Into valleys, long and wide,
Towards the ocean that is its goal,
Its journey travelled by our soul.
When I was but little boy,
The river rippled and dashed with joy,
And as I grew and longed to learn,

The river for the ocean yearned.
As young man travelled round the world,
The river twisted, turned and twirled,
Eager to find its resting place,
Eager to travel in time and space.

And as the seeking man grew older,
The river found the bigger boulders,
But on it travelled without care,
It knew its destiny's not there.

The rushing water's now quite slow,
The river old has nothing to show,
Its happiness is calm and deep,
As old man takes his final sleep.

The ocean that is never ending,
Is to the sky its waters lending,
To rain again on mountain top,
To make sure life's rivers never stop.

The rivers message lies in this
Ocean of Mercy, Peace and Bliss
It was getting dark and cold. It would be a cold night but the

sleeping bags that they had provided looked and felt warm. The girls came back and dinner was about to be served as the mountain peaks disappear into the night.

Guess what they served the girls for dinner? Chicken of course! That's what had happened to the missing chicken. The girls would not eat it but they were too embarrassed to say anything, so they threw it away and ate some of my vegetarian food. I realised as I started to doze off that I don't even know the names of our guide or cook.

16th October

It was quite cold and it rained during the night, but we were up at 7 AM for breakfast and ready to go.

I had been fell walking when I was at University 1969 to 1972; I had walked up Ben Nevis, Snowdon and several mountains in the Lake district including Skafell, Coniston and Helvellyn but I had not walked up many hills since then. I used to go caving and rock-climbing too. Used to, I stress..

We set out to walk to the tiny village of Aru, sometimes spelt Arru. It was lovely walk and fantastic scenery. I had thought it would be more difficult but mostly we walked on a road. We passed lots of small ganja plants, too small to harvest.

It rained again so we sheltered a while under trees and eventually reached Aru by 11.30. On the road we met a guy that Mary knew and when we got to Aru all his children were waiting for us. His house was the first house on the left! He invited us in for chai and a chance to dry off a bit.

He had about seven children of various ages, all beautiful. Well

I assumed they were all his.   We never saw the mother but granny was there, nodding and smiling at us.

We had to wait quite a time for Habib and our pony man.

Waiting For Habib
by
Alun Buffry

The folk in the village of Aru,
Had eyes fixed on us both like glue,
Their eyes shining, open wide,
As they're sitting side by side.

The granny's there, old, toothless and bent.
Her happy life is almost spent,
But still, just now and once a while,
She looked at us and gave a smile.

Whatever it was they were trying to say,
We never knew before on our way.
Their hospitality was ever so warm,
Amidst those mountains tall and calm.

We waited for three hours and more
Before Habib's donkey man we saw,
Then off we strode with just a wave,
To walk, eat and sleep midst memories saved.

For Roxana, Musaka a place called home.
For us it was a stepping stone.

After three and a half hours the ponies had still not arrived, so we walked back to the camp where the tents were already pitched again.

It was raining again, slightly, so we sat around the campfire and all was well.

The river was rushing now, the valley was luxurious, the mountain peaks were white with snow.

17th October.

We were up early and Habib was ready for us with breakfast; cornflakes, eggs, bread and chai.

The sun was shining on the mountain tops and creeping down the valley but neither Lizzy nor Mary ate breakfast, even though there was no chicken. Another chicken had disappeared.

We walked back to Aru where we mounted our ponies and rode most of the way to Lidderwat.

When I got on my pony it seemed to stumble on the stones; I

31

dismounted, thinking I was too heavy for it, being about ten stone. Habib said no, get back up. He said the ponies play games and if I did not ride it, it would always try to pretend I was too heavy and stumble. After that, it was no problem even on the hilly rocky bits.

I expected Lidderwat to be a small village but in fact it was just two small wooden huts, one for us. The scenery around us was simply amazing. Snowy mountains and pine trees. The sun was shining and the sky a deep cloudless blue. It was autumn here, so there were green pines and golden and brown trees.

Lidderwat was about 6 miles from Aru. One could carry on to Kolahoi which is the highest glacier in Kashmir, but we were already about 9,000 feet above sea level so we decided not to go any further. We were not equipped to walk in the snow and the ponies, as we were told, did not like it.

The girls were not eating the chicken in the packed lunches. It's a shame that the birds died for nothing.

Riding the pony was fine. It seemed like they know where to go and compete to lead the way. Occasionally they started trotting to get in front and we collided.

As we arrived, three or four children rushed up from nowhere, asking for cigarettes. The pony man said they were charas and gave one to the oldest girl who broke it up and looked. Then they all ran off shouting in unison, I know not what. Then they were back again, whispering to each other, watching me write and Lizzy laying in the sunshine.

The wooden hut was named 'The Paradise Hotel'.

18th October

We were up at 6.30 and the sun was shining and sweeping down the hill.

Lizzy had constipation. We stayed there until after lunch then headed back to Pahalgam. From there we took a taxi back to Srinagar. I pledge to come here again.

Pahalgam was a small town, just a few streets with cars, coaches and ponies, almost like the wild west but without cowboys.

We were in a different room on the houseboat. Lizzy said she had ant bites all up her legs

19th October: Houseboat

I woke up feeling fed up. Not sure why. Suddenly I started to wish I was back in Norwich. I thought it was because I knew we only had a few days left here. I felt like I had been too long in Srinagar and not seen anywhere else except Delhi. It makes sense to stay somewhere a while to get to know it but even two weeks was not long enough and I loved to roam new places.

Lizzy was now coughing a lot, like she had bronchitis. But she would not listen to advice or take help.

The she told me that she had lost her bank card and rupees. Stupidly she had put them on her back pocket when riding the pony. So we were short of money to pay the bills. Mary said we could send the money later.

20th October

Last night the electricity was off all night and still off when we got up, but it was sunny again, which improved the mood.

Mary talked with Mr Baktoo about her marrying Ahmed. He told her his wife would want her to sign a statement in court to say that she would stay in Kashmir and only go away if given permission and that she would never ask for a divorce. Then she would talk with Ahmed and ask him what to do. Also she would have to wear Moslem clothes in the presence of the family and friends. Under modern law also Ahmed could take up to another six wives! Mr Baktoo said he would pay for them to go anywhere for two or three months but after that she had to stay in Kashmir or Delhi.

Lizzy asked Mr Baktoo to read her palm, which he said he would. He held her hand and said to think of a flower. Then he said "rose". He was correct. Now he was calling her his guru!

He said he was very rich and owns many houseboats but his peace comes from keeping his family happy. He said he went to bed at 8 PM and got up at 4 AM. That evening, after he had been talking to us, we could hear his wife calling him. He said he only had one wife as he was happy with her. I wondered if he had intended proposing to Lizzy.

I gave Habib a gift of my telescopic umbrella. He was very happy with that. He said "I hope it will rain soon".

Habib gave Lizzy a red coral necklace which Mr Baktoo said was good but "only cost two rupees". The bastard! He may be rich but he may be mean too. Maybe he will give her a gold one, after all, she was his guru!

21st October

It was getting cold at night so we had hot water bottles. The electricity went off again at 11 o'clock last night. We had spent most of the evening talking with Yussef about trekking, whilst he was drinking whiskey and moaning about people smoking hash. He drank a whole bottle. He said he had travelled to the UK overland, but the law was that after getting back to India one must stay for at least eighteen months. One way out, he said, was through Nepal..

Mr Baktoo said that he thought that the Ayatollah was a number one fool and that he and Iran were very bad because they fight fellow Moslem and the Koran says not to fight. Personally, I am never keen on talking religion or politics as it so often offends.

We heard that crowds had gathered in town because somebody

had seen a cobra. So we went into town to take a look at what all the excitement was about. We found the place quite easily and saw about two dozen people staring at a patch of ground; cars were stopping to take a look; apparently that had been going on for about a week; we saw no sign of any snakes. People were saying that there are four snakes underground but nobody there had actually seen any,

There had been a government order that the houseboats had to be moved about. Lake Nageen was to be for deluxe houseboats only, Lake Dal for class A and class B and some of the houseboats at the smelly Dal gate were actually on dry land and would have to be moved. The river below the Dal Gate bridge was not a pleasant sight or smell.

Nageen was cleaner than Dal. They were lucky there were few motor boats.

22nd October

We spent last night at the Perfume Garden houseboat on Lake Nageen. The bathrooms had sunken baths.

Back on our "own boat" playing scrabble, then off to town to try to buy rolling tobacco and skins for Lizzy.

23rd October

We heard that we were going to be flying to Delhi tomorrow.

Lizzy insisted that I bought some condoms so she could swallow some hash to take back to Norwich. I knew that would not be easy. We went into town and it was so hot, I just wanted to sit down and have a drink before going shopping. She started screaming at me to go now. I went into a cafe and she stormed off.

I went to several chemists to ask; I tried calling them condoms, Durex, French letters to no avail. Then a boy of about thirteen approached me and asked if he could help.

How could I explain what I wanted. So I asked for a pharmacy where they spoke English and he took me to one. I asked and the guy at the counter said "Ah, you want rubber Johnnies?". He went to the back of the shop and came back with quite large plain cardboard box which was full of condoms. He asked me "How many". I said "four" and the business was done.

I went back to the houseboat. Lizzy was asleep; I put the condoms in the bedroom cabinet drawer.

Later, when she woke and we were served dinner, she would not speak to me. Mary asked what her problem was and she said because I refused to help her. I said "Your condoms are in the drawer." That seemed to work, but she was still quiet all evening.

24th October

So after a long wait at Srinagar airport, followed by a short flight and taxi ride, we were back in Delhi and at the Himalayan Holidays Office with Farook. He phoned Kuwait Airlines to confirm our flight back to the UK without problems. He then booked us a room for the night.

At 4 AM we took a taxi to Delhi airport.

To be honest I am glad to be home although it was a great holiday and I am already thinking of returning to Kashmir with somebody else. Lizzy was not the ideal travelling companion.

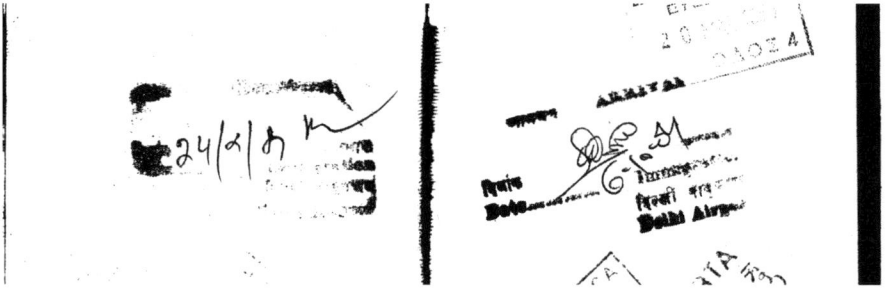

=====================

1985 India, Nepal and Kashmir with Lesley

13 March 1985: Delhi

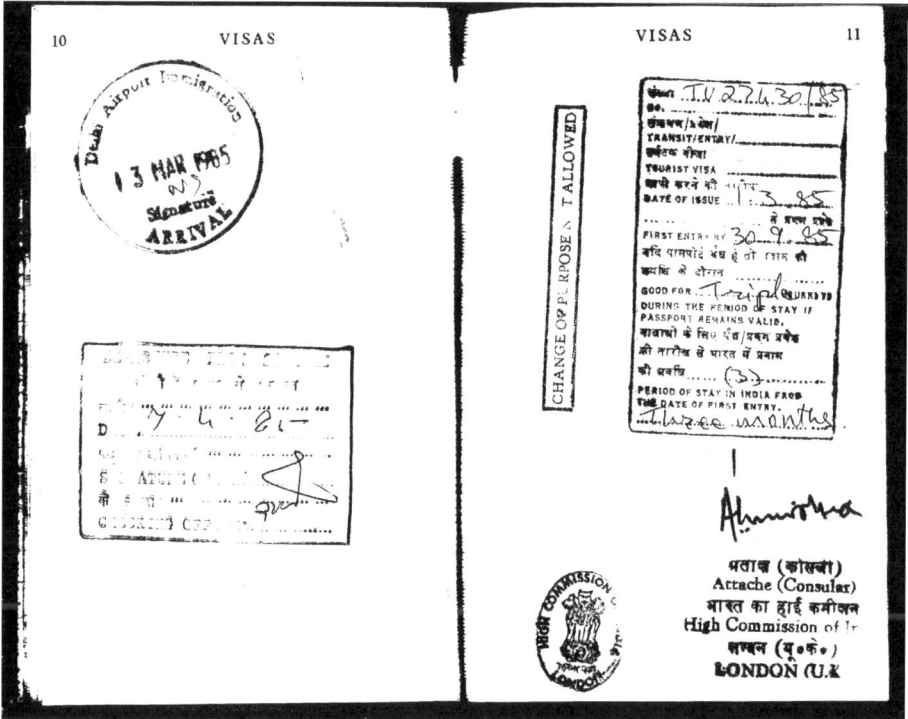

I had only known Lesley for a few months but we got on well. We had already been to London for a couple of days in order to buy our visas from the Indian Embassy, which was remarkably simple but involved staying overnight and going back to the Embassy the following day

Lesley and I arrived at Delhi airport just after midnight, after a reasonably comfortable eight-and-three-quarter hour flight from Heathrow with quite good food, free drinks and videos.

Naturally we were tired.

A soon as we left the plane the heat hit us like a hair drier, even at midnight. The first thought was to get to the hotel that had been booked for us by Himalayan Holidays rep Ali Baktoo, whom I had met in Kashmir the previous year.

But as soon as we left the airport, spotting no taxi available, we were approached by a three wheeler motor rickshaw, that they called a tuk-tuk and invited to board, "at cheap money", as he said, he had brought somebody to the airport from Delhi and needed a return fare. So in we jumped.

We gave the driver the address of the hotel.

"I am sorry Sir, but last night there was fire at that hotel so it is closed, so I take you to good cheap hotel."

I'd forgotten that tuk-tuk drivers were not bound by any oath to tell the truth. Rather so many were devoted to money, but we already on board so we stayed and said OK.

It took ages to get to Delhi. It was hot and the two of us with and our cases and bags but were pleased to arrive safely. It was Old Delhi and the hotel was called Natraj.

Of course, I would say, they were full so the only room left was in the attic, a small room with one bed, costing just 90 rupees, not a lot; it was clean but stuffy and we struggled to sleep.

In the morning we realised there was no breakfast here so we strolled down the dusty and dirty crowded street to find an eating place which turned out to be right next door, on Chitragupta Road. That sufficed so we quickly went back to Natraj which really should have been called Ratbag, freshened up and took a taxi into New Delhi to meet Ali at the Himalayan Holidays office.

Ali asked where we had been as our hotel had phoned him to say that we had not arrived. It had not had a fire after all. I should have known.

So he quickly booked us a room in a much better hotel and a taxi to Ratbag and back to get our luggage, then he said he would take us to our hotel and talk about our holiday, as we had not arranged anything at all. We had planned on eight to twelve weeks but had no confirmed flight home. So off we went, no problem at all.

After arriving at our hotel near Connaught Circus, we spent a few hours wandering about and eventually back to the office, where Ali said he could book us trips to Agra to see the Taj Mahal, the Fort and Fatepur Sikri. We would go by train and stay a few days. Then we would fly to Khajuraho to see the temples, fly on to Varanassi also called Benares, and back to Delhi. We would also travel to Jaiselmer in Rajasthan and go into the desert on camels, Nepal and Kashmir to stay on a luxury houseboat and go pony trekking. The price would include all transport, hotels and meals.

It was far more than we wanted to pay though, so thus started some hours of bartering, with changes to hotels and we would have to buy our own food except breakfast and on the houseboat and camel and pony trekking trips. We would also have to pay for our hotels in Nepal when we got there.

We settled on £1675 for the two of, not cheap but not bad as it covered eight weeks at least and included several stays in Delhi, plus we would have a few days in Delhi before taking the train to Agra.

That evening we felt honoured to eat dinner near the office, at the Baktoo home with Ali and his brother Yussef; spicy potatoes, rice, dahl, yogurt and Kashmir tea, eaten with our hands. The rice was put on our plates by hand and we took our own dahl and subji (vegetables) which we mixed with the rice with our fingers as did our hosts (right hands only – the left hand is used for unmentionable tasks like washing ones bum). It was quite delicious. We never met the women of the family. This was a Moslem house.

Our new hotel was the Ashok Yatri Niwas, Ashok Road, room 1027. This one we had to pay for, but that had to be in foreign currency or travellers cheques. Of course not as simple as it should have been as they said Lesley's signature did not match the one on the cheque, so next day we had to go to American Express to get cash in pounds.

14th March

We hardly left the hotel as we both felt exhausted. We ate just toast and lassi, the Indian Yoghurt drink for breakfast in the snack cafe downstairs, masala dosa for lunch. The tea was horrible. We strolled up and down Connaught circus, spotted a small restaurant where we would eat that evening, planned the next day and slept soundly.

15th March

In the morning we got out before it became unbearably hot again and took a ride to see The Red Fort, Lal Qila, constructed by the workers of Shah Jahan between 1638 and 1648. It was meant to be the centre of his new capital city but he never completely moved there from Agra because his son, Aurangzeb, deposed him and imprisoned him in Agra Fort. That was said to have been due to Shah Jahan having "wasted" too much money building the Taj Mahal as a mausoleum to his deceased wife and then planning to build a mirror image on the other side of the river.

The Emperor used to ride out of the Red Fort, on elephants, into the streets of Old Delhi (there was no New Delhi then), in a display of pomp and power.

It was beautiful place with incredible architecture, very peaceful and quiet, especially after the busy, noisy streets of Chandi Chowk.

The Jani Masjid mosque was huge, very crowded and surrounded by stalls, food houses and beggars. It was built 1644 to 1658. Huge wide steps rise to the mosque with four angled towers and two minarets, forty metres high, built from alternating red sandstone and white marble. The Mosque can hold up to 25,000 people. We did not go inside, something to do with Lesley's socks not being allowed!

Then we went to the Mahatma Gandhi museum, filled with newspaper clippings and items from his personal life. That also included one of the three bullets which had killed him and the blood-stained dhoti that he was wearing that day. The "Room of Violence" was quite disturbing, filled with pictures of suffering people. The Museum itself was dedicated to peace and entrance was free.

The Mahatmas ashes are nearby along with those of Nehru and of Indira Gandhi.

We took lunch at a dilapidated restaurant called Nirulas, opposite the museum and then went to the air conditioned underground bazaar just off Janpath, to buy some zips that Lesley wanted and ended up also buying her an outfit ready for

Rajasthan.

It was nearby, I think, where we were approached by a group of young women and teenage women, probably about eight of them, all smiling and asking for baksheesh. Sometimes we gave beggars a few small coins but this time not as there were so many. They crowded around us, especially Lesley. I gripped my shoulder bag tightly as we had to push our way through them. Later, Lesley realised that at least one hand had been inside her bag and stolen a small tin of Nivea hand cream and some make-up.

We took a tuk-tuk back to the hotel. On the roads I noticed so many forms of transport in one place: there were tuk-tuks, coaches and larger tuk-tuks, horses with traps, donkeys and men pulling carts, trucks, cars and even an elephant.

That evening we met up with Ali Baktoo again and he gave us our itinerary for the next two months, which we were well satisfied with, except there was not enough time, we felt, in Nepal. So he agreed to extend it to two weeks there and go to

Kashmir later.

I ate a decent vegetable Thali downstairs at Hotel Ashok Yatri Newas for fifteen rupees – getting used to the food now. Lesley had Sheesh Kebabs. Slept early that night so we could explore Delhi by ourselves the next day.

16th March

For breakfast I had an India pancake called a Dosa, filled with spicy vegetables and served with dips. Delicious!

That day we ended up spending most of the day inside the hotel as it was so hot outside, going out at 5 PM for a meal at Pot Pourri, Nimla's. I ate pizza and Lesley ate Mutton Tikka, with soda water drinks and banana split. That came to 80 rupees, just over three UK pounds. Afterwards we went to see Ali, drank some rum and played backgammon. I played against Ali and his brother Mohammed called Jimmy, who said he was unbeaten. I beat both of them several times. Ha!

18th March: AGRA

We arose at 5 AM to catch the 7.05 AM train, the Taj Express, to Agra, arriving at Agra Cantonment at 10.00 AM. Both stations were of course crowded.

As we left Agra Station we were approached by a smiling taxi driver who introduced himself as Maxi and offered to show us around at a "very good price" whilst we were there.

AGRAMAXI

by

Alun Buffry

We arrived in Agra and were led to a taxi,

49

By a smiling Moslem, name of Maxi,

Who took us all the sites to see,

Simple charges, a few rupees

You have to spend in every shop

Within which he took us to stop.

"Come in, sit down, don't walk past

"Look at my stones and see my brass,

"Quality friend you cannot be missing

"Excuse me Sir, I must do some wishing.

"You like some chai, cold drink, coffee?

"No don't talk now of your money!"

"Only to look and not to buy,

"See here it's cheap, and here is why -

"See the craftsmanship is fine,

"And it can be yours if you'll just sign

"The cheque or bill or pay in cash,

But first my friend, just smoke more hash!"

Maxi asked us for just 80 rupees for the whole day visiting the Taj Mahal, Agra Fort, the Mogul Palace. Our itinerary from the Baktoos included a one night stay at Hotel Amir, which looked clean, with a restaurant downstairs, free tea, a carpeted room with a shower and bath. Breakfast included cornflakes, already a treat!

Of course as well as site seeing, Maxi took us to shops, where of course he always earned a good commission despite our haggling. We bought rings, semi-precious gem stones including aquamarine, a marble inlaid table top (which, in 2021, I still have) some silk paintings and soapstone pieces. I thought that it I could sell them back in the UK it would go some way to paying for the holiday.

Agra Fort was a massive red fort, one third of which was open to the public; the rest was used by the Indian Army. Emperor Akbar started the building in 1565 and it was continued by his grandson, Shah Jahan. The one that built the Taj Mahal and was later overthrown by his own son Aurangzeb (Muhi-ud-Din Muhammad).

Inside the fort there were several palaces and also a beautiful and fine view of the Taj Mahal. The extensive walls were surrounded by two moats, one of which previously had been filled with water and the other with wild animals. One entered through the Amar Singh gate. The other gate, the Delhi gate, was used by the army.

The Moti Masjid, or Pearl Mosque, looked beautiful from the outside but was closed off.

The Hall of Public Audiences had amazing acoustics so that people even a hundred yards away (modern measurements of course) could hear the Emperor, even if he whispered.

The Hall of Private Audiences had two thrones, one for the Emperor and opposite that, one for his chief councillor. It was here that secret meetings were held under canvas. The Peacock Throne was kept here before it was later carried off to Tehran.

Jahangiri's Palace may be the most noteworthy building inside the Agra Fort. The Mahal was the principal zenana (palace for women belonging to the royal household), and was used mainly by the Rajput wives of Akbar. It was a form of Islamic architecture. The palace was built by Akbar. It was one of the earliest surviving buildings of Akbar's reign. Jahangir in his memoirs stated that the buildings were erected by his father Akbar but did not take any credit for the construction of Jahangiri palace. Mahal Mughal Empress Nur Jahan used this magnificent palace as her residence until her death on 17 December 1645. There was a huge bowl called Hauz-i-Jahangiri that was carved out of a single piece of stone. This was used as a container for fragrant rose water.

The Shish Mahal or Mirror Palace was once full of tiny mirrors and used by concubines.

The beautiful Grape Gardens (Anguri Bagh) probably never had grapes! Built by Shah Jehan in 1637, with Khas Mahal to its east and red sandstone arcades on the other three sides, it was the principal square of the zenana apartments or the living area of the royal ladies. There was a marble paved platform with a fountain in its centre and the garden itself was divided into compartments in intricate geometrical pattern.

In front of the Jahangiri's Palace, there was a huge bath, about 5 feet deep, carved out of a single piece of stone. Underneath was a cool room used in summertime, and above it was a white marble palace. When the Emperor Jahan's wife died and she was buried at the Taj Mahal, it was closed up so nobody could see the detail and care taken in building this masterpiece.

One entered the grounds through a sandstone arch inscribed from the Koran. A watercourse runs from there through the gardens to the Taj Mahal.

The shops of Agra offered a variety of fine crafted goods. The marble shop had table tops of marble inlaid with slivers of semi precious stones, boxes, table mats, lamp stands, chess boards and much more. Some of the work was very detailed. The patterns were drawn on the marble and the shapes cut out and filled. Much of the work was done by children. The gem shop contained many precious and semi precious stones, with Star of India, Black Stars, Lapis Lazuli, Aquamarine and Tigers Eye, of fine, medium and poor quality, sold at rupees per carat. They would place a stone in a ring or almost anywhere else you want it. For a price! They also sold silk paintings, inlaid bags and belts and small items. There was also a sitar shop with beer, charas and music. Small sitars were from £35 to £50, larger single drum £100 to £200, and a beautiful double drum for £400. They said sitar was easy to learn how to play. The bulbous part was made from pumpkin.

This beautiful copper and white brass pot is 21 inches tall.

The brass shop was piled high with lots of shelves with many brass items. The most impressive were the copper and white brass coffee pots in various sizes, many inlaid with semi precious stones. I bought one lovely piece about fifteen inches tall, with a decorated handle and dragon-like headed spout. I still have it to this day. It was to be shipped back to the UK along with the many other items that I bought with the intention of selling. These included many wind chimes of small brass bells with shapes of animals or birds or letters spelling out words such as LOVE and PEACE. They were sold by the weight. Also several beautiful enamelled brass vases and lamp stands, a wine set consisting of a tray, decanter and goblets, various ashtrays shaped like playing cards, hearts, diamonds, clubs and spades, brass lighter covers and several coloured enamelled brass bowls of different sizes.

That evening we ate at Zorba the Buddha: clean with a good selection of vegetarian food. It was run by Sanyasi. The Sanyassen were dressed in orange it was an unusual modern cult of devotees that had relinquished their possessions but did not seem limited to any particular lifestyle or ritual either. Still, they seemed happy so good luck to them. I had met some back in Norwich. Most of them smoked chillums of hash.

19th March

I had been in Agra in 1972 and visited the Taj Mahal and Fatepur Sikri, both wonderful. At that time, I had stayed in Government Rest House on the outskirts of Agra and got around by bicycle rickshaw and buses. Fatepur Sikri was where we were heading, by taxi with Maxi.

There were four obvious differences between 1972 and now, 1985. The streets were more crowded with local people, rickshaws and much more motorised traffic and correspondingly noisier and dustier. There were far more tourists and hasslers. There was more electricity and more telephones. Everyone seemed much more in a rush.

We made quite an early start. Maxi was waiting for us outside our hotel. I was beginning to wonder whether he was simply a profiteering but friendly taxi driver or some sort of Government employee to keep a watchful and caring eye over us. We soon arrived at the Taj.

This was from a guide book:

"The Taj Mahal or Crown of the Palace was built from white marble and was on the southern bank of the river Yamuna. It was considered to be one of the most beautiful buildings in the world. It was commissioned in 1632 by the Mughal emperor Shah Jahan (reigned from 1628 to 1658) to house the tomb of his favourite wife, Mumtaz Mahal who died on 17 June 1631 while giving birth to their 14th child, Gauhara Begum; it also houses the tomb of Shah Jahan himself. The tomb was the centrepiece of a 17-hectare (42-acre) complex, which includes a mosque and a guest house, and was set in formal gardens bounded on three sides by a defensive battlement.

"The tomb was the central focus of the entire complex of the Taj Mahal. It was a large, white marble structure standing on a square plinth and consists of a symmetrical building with an

iwan (an arch-shaped doorway) topped by a large dome. Like most Mughal tombs, the basic elements are Persian in origin. The base structure was a large multi-chambered cube with bevelled corners forming an unequal eight-sided structure that was approximately 180 feet on each of the four long sides.

"The most spectacular feature was the marble dome that surmounts the tomb. The dome was nearly 115 feet high which was close in measurement to the length of the base, and accentuated by the cylindrical "drum" it sits on, which was approximately 23 feet high. Because of its shape, the dome was often called an onion dome or amrud (guava dome). The top was decorated with a lotus design which also serves to accentuate its height. The shape of the dome was emphasised by four smaller domed kiosks placed at its corners, which replicate the onion shape of the main dome. The dome was slightly asymmetrical. It's columned bases open through the roof of the tomb and provide light to the interior. Tall decorative spires extend from edges of base walls, and provide visual emphasis to the height of the dome.

"The main finial section of the roof was originally made of gold but was replaced by a copy made of gilded bronze in the early 19th century. This feature was a clear example of integration of traditional Persian and Hindu decorative elements. The finial was topped by a moon, a typical Islamic motif whose horns point heavenward.

"The minarets, which are each more than 130 feet tall, display the designer's penchant for symmetry. They were designed as working minarets, a traditional element of mosques, used by the muezzin to call the Islamic faithful to prayer. Each minaret was effectively divided into three equal parts by two working balconies that ring the tower. At the top of the tower was a final balcony surmounted by a chattri that mirrors the design of

those on the tomb. The chattris all share the same decorative elements of a lotus design topped by a gilded finial. The minarets were constructed slightly outside of the plinth so that in the event of collapse, a typical occurrence with many tall constructions of the period, the material from the towers would tend to fall away from the tomb.

"The exterior decorations of the Taj Mahal are among the finest in Mughal architecture. As the surface area changes, the decorations are refined proportionally. The decorative elements were created by applying paint, stucco, stone inlays or carvings. In line with the Islamic prohibition against the use of anthropomorphic forms, the decorative elements can be grouped into either calligraphy, abstract forms or vegetative motifs. Throughout the complex are passages from the Koran that comprise some of the decorative elements.

"The calligraphy on the Great Gate reads "O Soul, thou art at rest. Return to the Lord at peace with Him, and He at peace with you." The calligraphy was created in 1609 by a calligrapher named Abdul Haq. Shah Jahan conferred the title of "Amanat Khan" upon him as a reward for his "dazzling virtuosity." Near the lines from the Qur'an at the base of the interior dome was the inscription, "Written by the insignificant being, Amanat Khan Shirazi." Higher panels are written in slightly larger script to reduce the skewing effect when viewed from below.

"The interior chamber of the Taj Mahal reaches far beyond traditional decorative elements. The inlay work was a lapidary of precious and semiprecious gemstones. The inner chamber was an octagon with the design allowing for entry from each face, although only the door facing the garden to the south was used. The interior walls are about 82 feet high and are topped by a "false" interior dome decorated with a sun motif. The four central upper arches form balconies or viewing areas, and each balcony's exterior window had an intricate screen cut from marble. In addition to the light from the balcony screens, light enters through roof openings covered by chattris at the corners. The octagonal marble screen bordering the cenotaphs was made from eight marble panels carved through with intricate pierce work. The remaining surfaces are inlaid in delicate detail with semi-precious stones forming twining vines, fruits and flowers. Each chamber wall was highly decorated with dado bas-relief, intricate lapidary inlay and refined calligraphy panels which reflect, in little detail, the design elements seen throughout the exterior of the complex.

"Muslim tradition forbids elaborate decoration of graves. Hence, the bodies of Mumtaz and Shah Jahan were put in a relatively plain crypt beneath the inner chamber with their faces turned right, towards Mecca. Mumtaz Mahal's cenotaph was placed at the precise centre of the inner chamber on a rectangular marble base.

"The complex is set around a large square garden that uses raised pathways that divide each of the four-quarters of the garden into 16 sunken flowerbeds. Halfway between the tomb and gateway in the centre of the garden was a raised marble water tank with a reflecting pool positioned on a north-south axis to reflect the image of the mausoleum. The elevated marble water tank was called al Hawd al-Kawthar in reference to the "Tank of Abundance" promised to Mohammed."

That reflection was really beautiful. From the far end there were always people taking photographs.

When we left the Taj, Maxi was waiting for us with two cups of tea, some small cakes and a bottle of water. He seemed anxious to take us to our next stop, Fatepur Sikri, about 20 miles and over an hour away.

Fatepur Sikri

Fatepur Sikri, which as I said I had also visited in 1972, this time had other tourists strolling around on the various levels. It may not have been as immediately visually impressive as the Taj but was a fascinating place to see.

"The city itself was founded as the capital of Mughal Empire in 1571 by Akbar, serving this role from 1571 to 1585, when Akbar abandoned it due to a campaign in the Punjab and was later completely abandoned in 1610 due partly to a shortage of

63

good water.

"It's a massive complex on several levels surrounded by a five mile wall on three sides and a lake on the other. Entrance was through a series of gates, namely, Delhi Gate, the Lal Gate, the Agra Gate and Birbal's Gate, Chandanpal Gate, The Gwalior Gate, the Tehran Gate, the Chor Gate, and the Ajmeri Gate."

64

It was quite confusing inside, up and down the various levels, so we did not get to see it all, with no guide.

"The emperor Akbar tried to start a new religion here, called Deen Illahi, a synthesis of several religions of that time.

"Inside the walled area, are palaces such as Jodh Bai, used by Akbar. The court ladies used to sit here watching the goings on below Bhirbal Bhavan.

"Some of the important buildings in this city, both religious and secular are:

Fatepur Sikri, India

"Buland Daewaz: Set into the south wall of congregational mosque, the Buland Darwaza at Fatehpur Sikri was 180 feet high, from the ground, gradually making a transition to a human scale in the inside. The gate was added around five years after the completion of the mosque to commemorate Akbar's successful Gujarat campaign. It carries two

inscriptions in the archway, one of which reads: "Isa, Son of Mariam said: The world is a bridge, pass over it, but build no houses on it. He who hopes for an hour may hope for eternity. The world endures but an hour. Spend it in prayer, for the rest is unseen".

"*The central portico comprises three arched entrances, with the largest one, in the centre, was known locally as the Horseshoe Gate, after the custom of nailing horseshoes to its large wooden doors for luck. Outside the giant steps of the Buland Darwaza to the left was a deep well.*

"*Jama Masjod was a Jama Mosque meaning the congregational mosque and was perhaps one of the first buildings to be constructed in the complex, with a massive entrance to the courtyard, the Buland-Darwaza added some five years later. It was built in the manner of Indian mosques around a central courtyard. A distinguishing feature was the row of chhari over the sanctuary. Chhatri are elevated, dome-*

shaped pavilions used as an element in Indian architecture. The word literally means "canopy" or "umbrella." There were three mihrabs, raised platforms, in each of the seven bays, while the large central mihrab was covered by a dome and it was decorated with white marble inlay of geometric patterns.

"The Tomb of Salim Chishti was a white marble encased tomb of the Sufii (1478–1572), within the Jama Masjid's courtyard. The single-storey structure was built around a central square chamber, within which was the grave of the saint, under an ornate wooden canopy encrusted with mother-of-pearl mosaic. Surrounding it was a covered passageway for walking round in a circle with carved stone pierced screens all around with intricate geometric design and an entrance to the south.

"On the left of the tomb, to the east, stands a red sandstone tomb of Islam Khan, son of Shaikh Badruddin Chisti and grandson of Shaikh Salim Chishti, who became a general in the Mughal army in the reign of Jahangir. The tomb was topped by a dome and thirty-six small domed Chattris and contained a number of graves, some unnamed,that were all male descendants of Shaikh Salim Chishti.

"Diwan-i-Aam or Hall of Public Audience, was a building typology found in many cities where the ruler meets the general public. In this case, it was a pavilion-like multi-bayed rectangular structure fronting a large open space. South west of the Diwan-i-Am and next to the Turkic Sultana's House stand Turkic Baths.

"Diwan-i-Khas or Hall of Private Audience, was a plain square building with four chattris on the roof. However it was famous for its central pillar, which had a square base and an octagonal shaft, both carved with bands of geometric and floral designs, further its thirty-six serpentine brackets support a circular platform for Akbar, which was connected to each corner of the building on the first floor, by four stone walkways. It was here that Akbar had representatives of different religions discuss their faiths and gave private audience.

"IIbadaht Khana or House of Worship was a meeting house built in 1575 CE by the Mughal Emperor Akbar.

"Anup Talao: Anup Talao was built by Raja Anup Singh Sikarwar, an ornamental pool with a central platform and four bridges leading up to it. Some of the important buildings of the royal enclave are surround by it including, Khwabgah (House of Dreams) Akbar's residence, Panch Mahal, a five-storey palace, Diwan-i-Khas (Hall of Private Audience), Ankh Michauli and the Astrologer's Seat, in the south-west corner of the Pachisi Court.

"Hujra-i-Anup Talao: It was said to be the residence of Akbar's Muslim wife, although this was disputed due to its small size.

"Mariam-uz-Zamani's Palace was the building of Akbar's Rajput wives, was built around a courtyard, with special care being taken to ensure privacy.

"Naubat Khana, also known as Naggar Khana, meaning a drum house, where musician used drums to announce the arrival of the Emperor. It was situated ahead of the Hathi Pol Gate or the Elephant Gate, the south entrance to the complex, suggesting that it was the imperial entrance.

"The Pachisi Court was a square marked out as a large board game, the precursor to modern day Ludo game where people served as the playing pieces.

"Panch Mahal was a five-storied palatial structure, with the tiers gradually diminishing in size, till the final one, which was a single large-domed Chattri. Originally pierced stone screens faced the facade and probably sub-divided the interior as well, suggesting it was built for the ladies of the court. The floors are supported by intricately carved columns on each level, totalling to 176 columns in all.

"Birbal's House, the house of Akbar's favourite minister, who was a Hindu. Notable features of the building are the horizontal sloping sunshades and the brackets which support them.

"The impressive Hiran Minar, or Elephant Tower, was a circular tower covered with stone projections in the form of elephant tusks. Traditionally it was thought to have been erected as a memorial to the Emperor Akbar's favourite elephant. However, it was probably a used as a starting point for subsequent mileposts.

69

"Other buildings included Taksal (mint), Daftar Khana (Records Office), Karkhana (Royal Workshop), Khazana Treasury), Hammam (Turkic Baths), Darogha's quarters, stables, caravanserai and such."

Whilst we were there we were approached by a family of about 15 who insisted on having a photograph with me, which Lesley took. Not all of them wanted to be in it, but it's a great pic that I still have and I promised to send a copy which I did when we got back to Norwich and had the films developed. There were no digital cameras in 1985.

Well that was a whole lot to remember so I copied the information from the pamphlets.

20th March: Khajuraho

After a whole day of sightseeing, we were of course well worn out, but nevertheless we were up and on our way to Agra airport and there by 7 AM. After about an hour of hassling, our seats were finally confirmed and we boarded the 737 for Khajuraho, a flight of just 40 minutes. We took a taxi to our five star hotel, which had a large double room with hot and cold water. We rested a while then had lunch of vegetable curry, dahl, rice and chapati with lassi drink and chai, for me and mutton biriani for Lesley. Then we walked across the road to see the Western group of temples.

Those temples were built in the tenth century and mostly in good condition with thousands of small statues. Some were damaged with bits that were missing because they had been cut off and sold. Most were built between the tenth and twelfth centuries. Exactly why they were built here, nobody knows. The remoteness and isolation of Khajuraho probably helped preserve them.

The site seemed remarkably quiet and peaceful after the hustles and bustles of Delhi and Agra. We both loved it there and there were no hustlers at all.

Each temple had a three or five part plan. One enters a temple through a porch behind which was a hall which leads to the main hall. It was supported by columns. A vestibule leads to the inner sanctum or garbhagriha.

Outside each temple was layered with statues of people in various poses, many explicitly sexual, fighting, hunting, processions, an orgy scene and more, even a man having sex with a horse, going up to higher towers that top the inner sanctums.

73

The entrances face east so they catch the light inside.

The blocks were carved together with no use of mortar and made from sandstone carried from about 20 miles away.

"The Lakshmana Temple, built 930 to 950 AD, was dedicated to Vaikuntha Vishnu, an aspect of the god Vishnu. It is the best preserved of the temples in this complex. "The wall portion was studded with balconied windows with ornate balustrades. It had two rows of sculptures (refer images of temple's outer wall) including divine figures, couples and erotic scenes. The sanctum doorway is of seven sakhas (vertical panels). The central one being decorated with the ten incarnations of Vishnu. The Lintel depicts goddess Lakshmi in the centre flanked by the gods Brahma and Vishnu. The sanctum contains four-armed sculpture of Vishnu. One of the niches had the image of the sculptor and his disciples at work. The Main image is of tri-headed and four-armed sculpture of Vaikuntha Vishnu, The central head represented a human and two sides of boar.

"Behind the temples is a beautiful flowered garden, quiet and serene with the temples built on one base. The largest and most ornate is the Kandariya Mahadeu, built 1025 to 1050 AD, 100 feet high with 226 statues inside and 646 statues outside, mostly about three feet in height."

An incredible amount of work and admirable skills. They are in three bands, goddesses, women and erotic scenes. Some of the positions depicted would surely win prizes in the sex Olympics.

"In the interior space from the entrance there are three mandapas or halls, which successively rise in height and width, which was inclusive of a small chamber dedicated to Shiva, a chamber where the Shiva linga, the phallic emblem of Shiva was deified. The sanctum was surrounded by interlinked passages which also have side and front balconies. Due to inadequate natural light in the balconies the sanctum had very little light thus creating a "cave like atmosphere" which was in total contrast to the external parts of the temple. Women walk

75

round that and sit on it and say a prayer for pregnancy. In the interior halls of the temple and on its exterior faces there are elaborately carved sculptures of gods and goddesses, musicians and nymphs. The huge pillars of the halls have architectural features of the "vine or scroll motif". In the corners of the halls there are insets which are carved on the surface with incised patterns. There was a main tower above the sanctum and there are two other towers above the other mantapas also in the shape of "semi-rounded, stepped, pyramidal form with progressively greater height". The main tower was encircled by a series of interlinked towers and spires of smaller size. These are in the form of a repeated subset of miniature spires that abut a central core which gives the temple an unevenly cut contour similar to the shape of a mountain range of mount Kailasa where the god Shiva resides, which was appropriate to the theme of the temples here.

"The exterior surfaces of the temples are entirely covered with

sculptures in three vertical layers. Here, there are horizontal ribbons carved with images, which shine bright in the sun light, providing rhythmic architectural features. Among the images of gods and heavenly beings, Agri, the god of fire was prominent. They are niches where erotic sculptures are fitted all round which are a major attraction among visitors. Some of these erotic sculptures are very finely carved and are in mithuna (coitus) postures with maidens flanking the couple, which was a frequently noted motif. There was also a "male figure suspended upside" in coitus posture, a kind of yogic pose, down on his head. The seven fearful protector goddesses include: Brahmi seated on a swan of Brahma ; Maheshwari with three eyes seated on Shiva's bull, Nandi; Kumari; Vaishnavi mounted on Garuda, the boar-headed Varahi, Narasimhi; the lion-headed and Chamunda, the slayer of demons Chanda and Munda. The image of Sardula, a mythical creature with lion face and human limbs in lower panel was a unique figure seen in the temple.

"Next to this temple is Mahadeva temple which was largely defaced, and the smaller Jagadamba. They were originally dedicated to Vishnu, but now to Kali or Parvati. Inside was the blackened female goddess.

"Nearby is the Chitagupta temple, lighter in colour, dedicated to Surya, the Sun God. Here we saw statues of dancing girls, processions and elephant fighting. In the southern wall was a statue of the eleven-headed Vishnu. Inside was Surya with his seven-headed horse.

"The Parvati Temple is in front of the others and mainly ruined. It was dedicated to Vishnu and had sculptures of Ganga, the river god, riding a crocodile, and Yamuna, a river god, riding a turtle.

"The Vishnu and Nandi Temple was built about 1000 AD. A five part design with a statue of Shiva's bull, Nandi facing it outside. There are high steps flanked by lions and elephant statues. Also we see sculptures of a woman holding a baby, another combing her hair, another putting on makeup with a mirror and some in Playboy-like poses."

We visited the nearby museum which contains fine images of gods, Vishnu, Buddha and an elephant god with six arms.

That was enough for us. There are two other groups of temples which we did not see,

21st March

That day we were supposed to take a flight to Varanasi.

We got up at 7 AM and took a taxi to the airport.

Guess what! The plane was full! So back we went to the Indian Airways office at the Hotel Temple and plan to give it another try tomorrow after being promised seats, that we had paid for. We were on a waiting list. "No problem Sir, see you later! God wants you to stay!"

We were a bit pissed off but will get to see more sites.

This was when we met Rameshwar, supposedly an official government guide, who wanted to stick to us like glue as if keeping an eye on us. We spent most of the day with him.

22nd March

Again no seats on the plane, so we had to stay another night, this time at the house of Rameshwar and his family: wife and children, mother and elder brother.

First we went going with him to see the Jain Temples.

"Two of the large temples still stand in a good state of preservation in the original form. The portico of the Adinath temple was a later addition. The enclosed Shantinath temple, just 100 years old. It houses a massive monolithic Shantinath image. It also incorporates at least one other Chandella period temple."

I smoked a chillum with a monk at one of the Jain temples, very little tobacco, from a roasted cigarette then moistened with dew from a plant nearby and rubbed in his hand. It was a hot, dry smoke but very effective. Nice!

79

It was an extremely and uncomfortably hot day. Rameshwar kept wanting to take us one at time on the back of his scooter, trying to split us up. Obviously I was not at all happy about this.

He persuaded Lesley to go first to see a waterfall, despite my warnings. He was supposed to come back to get me within 30 minutes but time was passing and it was well over an hour and no sign of them. I was glad I got him to write his name and address in my notebook. It's worrying but what could I do? I couldn't really call police or anybody at this stage, it would end out being a problem either way. I was sure that I would have to pay. So it was a matter of lazing around, waiting.

The creep brought Lesley back a few hours later. She said the waterfall was dried up so had taken her to a lake. She had no idea where she was. Later she told me he tried to kiss her and threatened to throw himself into the lake. Shame he didn't, but no harm done.

That evening Rameshwar wanted us to go to another lake. He said would we go for a walk with his children but when I said OK he said I would walk with them and he would take Lesley and unbelievably she said yes. I said no, we all go together, so he promised to take her and come back in ten minutes. He said he would take us to see his "other Babu", whatever that means. Then we were all going together. The journey took about fifteen minutes, so there was no way he could have come back in ten.

We went to a small cinema that was packed, showing a film in Hindi, just local people. Before I even knew it, Lesley was gone again. So I went outside to look for her. I did not find her at that time though. Rameshwar had said that he would take her first and come back in ten minutes. I said "no chance", so we all went together, walking; it was not very far. It was just dimly lit back streets in a village. Actually it was a waste of time, just a house with young women and a few guys. I wonder if it was a brothel.

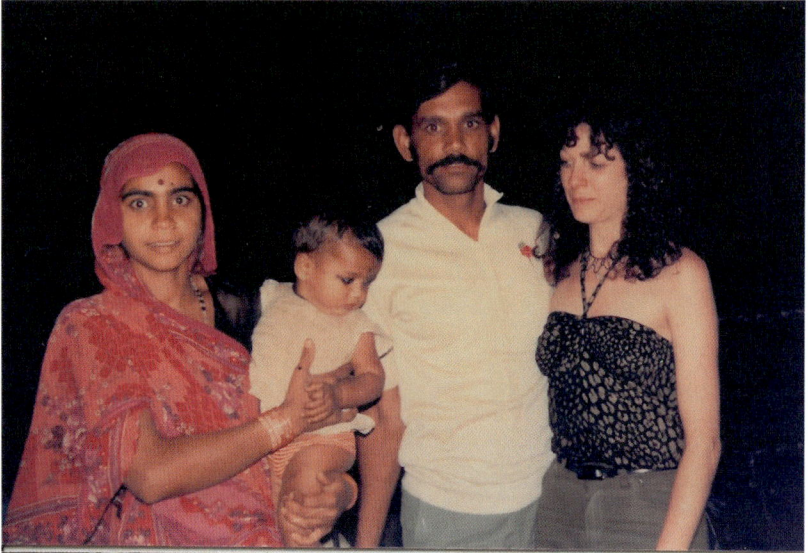

We were soon back at Rameshwar's house where we met his family.

There was a strange vibe from the elderly mother. I found out that she was upset because Lesley had not touched her feet. Lesley said she would not do that but I persuaded her that it was a custom and sign of respect, so she did. Remeshwar's brother went to change his shirt, so we could take photos; "but no touching", he said.

Rameshwar offered us a separate bedroom with a small bed; I slept on the floor. I put a chair up against the door in case anyone tries to come in during the night. Lesley said not to do that as they will feel insulted. I said that they would not know unless they tried the door.

Sure enough, early morning, somebody tried to come in.

23rd March: Varanasi and Sarnath

A while later when we were up and dressed, Rameshwar said his wife asked did we fuck on the bed!

So back to the airport again, hoping for a flight – third time lucky?

Varanasi was 88 degree Fahrenheit, that's 31 degree centigrade but it felt even hotter as we left the airport just before noon. We took a taxi into town to our hotel and ended up booking some tours to see temples.

Sanarth, about 6 miles away, was lovely, calm and peaceful. It was said that the actual Buddha came here to preach, in what was now a deer park. It was close to where the river Ganges and the river Varuna meet.

"Sarnath had been variously known as Mrigadava, Migadāya, Rishipattana and Isipatana throughout its long history. Mrigadava means "deer-park". "Isipatana" was the name used in the Pali Canon, collection of scriptures in the Theraveda Buddhist tradition and means the place where holy men landed.

"The legend says that when the Buddha-to-be was born, some devas (heavenly beings) came down to announce it to 500 rishis. Another explanation for the name was that Isipatana was so-called because, sages, on their way through the air (from the Himalayas), alight here or start from here on their aerial flight.

"Before Gautama (the Buddha-to-be) attained enlightenment, he gave up his austere penances and his friends, the Pañcavaggiya monks. Seven weeks after his enlightenment under the Bodhi tree in Bodhi Gaya, Buddha left Umvela and travelled to Isipatana to rejoin them because, using his spiritual

powers, he had seen that his five former companions would be able to understand Dharma quickly. While travelling to Sarnath, Gautama Buddha had no money to pay the ferryman to cross the Ganges, so he crossed it through the air.

"Ashok, a Buddhist emperor, erected monuments and stupas there.

"Sarnath was once populated by 1500 priests and monks and the main stupa was 328 feet high. A stupa ("stupa" was Sanskrit for heap) was an important form of Buddhist

architecture, though it predates Buddhism. It was generally considered to be a place of burial or a receptacle for religious objects. At its simplest, a stupa was a dirt burial mound faced with stone."

"The Dhamekh Stupa was about 500 AD, said to be on top of a previous construction. It had geometrical floral patterns.

"In front of the main shrine stands the Ashoki Pillar which once stood about 60 feet high and had four faces of lions. It was a museum. There are four creatures: the lion representing bravery, an elephant symbolising Buddha's mother's dream, a horse representing Buddha's journey from home on horseback and a bull.

"The Dhamek Stupa is an impressive structure, 128 feet high and 93 feet in diameter.

"The Chaukhandi Stupa commemorates the spot where the Buddha met his first disciples, dating back to the fifth century or earlier and later enhanced by the addition of an octagonal tower of Islamic origin."

There was also a Bodhi tree planted by said to have been grown from a cutting of the Bodhi Tree at Bodh Gaya.

Also there was the Maha Bodhi Society Temple containing Japanese frescoes of Buddha's life.

It was certainly tranquil on the site and we spent some time just sitting in the shade of a tree.

Now we were back in town with its crowded streets of dustiness and noise, and off to see the Durga Temple and the Monkey Temple where monkeys hang out. Durga is the goddess of power and a terrifying form of Shiva's consort Parvati. "You can look inside but you cannot go in", we were told. So we took a peep. Outside was a pool of very smelly water where pilgrims wash! Also goats were sacrificed here at festivals. We were told that years ago children were also sacrificed here. Hinduism is not at all like Buddhism. I much prefer Buddhism, devoid of gods and bloody sacrificial rituals.

The new Vishwaneth Temple was however open to visitors. It was a replica of the original temple. Inside was a Shiva lingam. Women wanting pregnancy were supposed to strip and sit astride the lingam several times, praying for a baby. I don't know if that worked but pretty sure they would also need a man.

"The Bharat Mata Mandir, or Mother India Temple, was erected by Mahatma Gandi. Anyone can enter and inside was a map of India and the Himalayas, Bay of Bengal and Shri Lnka (also known as Ceylon). You can go down some steps and view it from there."

To be honest, we were both getting fed up being led around by guides or government spies or whatever they are, even though it helped to have somebody explain things to us. That day we were thankful that the guide just said goodbye but often we ended up drinking chai or lemonade in a shop. The shop staff were very good at getting sales when we had no intention or buying anything to start with. They were very polite and jolly, taking time to carefully show each piece as if it were a treasure, then asking which we like best. Then the inevitable bartering. One had to be careful not to buy stuff that we would not have room in our luggage to take home. But the quality of the goods was also excellent and prices cheap.

On the way back to the hotel we spotted several Naga (naked Sadhu) strolling down the street. Meanwhile, even being clothed, we were both suffering from mosquito bites. Lesley had reacted badly to them and was scratching.

24th March.

Trying to Fly and Wondering Why.
by

Alun Buffry

Varanasi airport is quite a dump.

It's run by a man who is quite a chump.

Now we cannot board the plane.

Later we will miss our train.

Money flowing down the drain,

India Airways fucked my brain.

Seems the way here is to cheat,

So the system you can beat,

Just don't let them squash your feet,

Push for schedules try to keep.

"Baksheesh - don't say that word here sir,

We're all paid well by Indian Air "

And "you don't know the system here."

Well I think it fucking weird!

In India, it's different, so we're told,

Totally corrupt since times of old.

No problem sir, your seats we've sold,

Paid in Karma but now with gold.

We were supposed to be flying back to Delhi this day, to catch a train. That didn't happen. So we flew back another day late

25th March: Back to Delhi

Back in Delhi a day late so we had missed our train to Rajasthan. Ali Baktoo tried to get us a flight, to no avail, so we would go by train later.

In the meantime, we made a visit to Delhi Zoo.

The zoo contained a wide variety of birds, buffalo, deer and donkeys. There was also an elephant house where we had a private visit. Lesley was pleased to pat and befriend an elephant. He probably remembers Lesley until this day.

Then we went to Connaught Circus where Lesley had her shoes re-heeled, and then a nearby park where I reluctantly surrendered to a massage.

All of a sudden that evening, we found ourselves rushing to Old Delhi railway station where we picked up tickets and squashed into a second class department.

The carriage compartment was meant for eight but there were twelve of us trying to sit down.

As this was an overnight train, we wondered how we would ever sleep. But later a guard came along and got some people to leave and we climbed up the three tiers to our uncomfortable beds.

We arrived in Jodhpur at 11.30 AM and catch another train to Jaiselmer.

26th March Jodhpur

Breakfast on the train consisted of two vegetable cutlets, toast and tea or coffee. It was jerky ride, constantly stopping and starting, probably due to cows on the line. Cows are considered very Holy in India and a train killing or harming one would be regarded very seriously.

Outside the window we could see the countryside was becoming more and more parched, with just a few trees and camels, a few goats and chickens here and there near small settlements and villages.

Lesley was now covered with mosquito bites which she had scratched raw, so her arms were covered with red blotches and people were noticeably keeping their distance!

When we arrived in Jodhpur it was incredibly hot, far too hot to go site seeing to the famous fort.

First we had to get a new ticket to Jaiselmer as the other one was for yesterday and then discovered we could only get a refund back in Delhi (thanks Ali) We managed to get first class.

We spent some time that afternoon wandering the streets and Lesley went off to buy me some Indian white cotton pyjamas. I had a delicious thick lime lassi drink in the Agra Sweet Home opposite the Sojati Gate. Inside the gate there were long, winding streets full of small shops, rows selling cloths and clothes, rows selling clocks.

Jodpur Station, India

27th March: Jaiselmer

The night train to Jaiselmer arrived at 7.30 AM. It was already quite hot but bearable. However by the time we had taken chai, all the taxis were gone, so we had to phone the manager at out Hotel Fort View and he sent a taxi to pick us up.

The hotel was superb, with a very friendly and helpful manager and, best of all, an incredible view of the beautiful town and fort. Although the rooms were basic, with twin beds and shower downstairs, it feels good here. He explained the best times to see the sites and told us all about our three day camel trek in the desert. He also confirmed our train tickets back to Delhi on 2nd April.

By 10.30 it was much hotter so we decided to hang out in and near the hotel and take a stroll later. So far Jaiselmer looked like a dream or something from Arabian Nights. The fort was quite magnificent, built in 1156 by Rawal Jaisal on top the 260 feet Trikuta Hill. About a quarter of the population lived within it. Also within was a seven storey palace.

Jaiselmer was once an important stopping place for rich merchants travelling from Karachi and then here by camel and on to Delhi and all over India until the port of Bombay opened up. The population at that time was 20,000. Jodhpur had 400,000 people living there.

There were many shops selling, amongst other things, silk paintings and dresses which I knew I could sell easily back home, so a visit to some was on the itinerary, but not that day. I did buy a long piece of bright yellow cotton to wrap round my head for when we did our safari. We also bought light clothing for the days, warmer for the evenings, water bottles and plenty of purification pills and my camera. When we left we would be travelling with a camel riding boy, a guide and a cook. They will provide our meals and comforts and we would sleep under the stars.

28th March

Up and ready to go at 6AM, whilst it was still comparatively cool. My breakfast was cornflakes Indian style, toast and chai. There were lots of pigeons and other birds about.

Sitting on the camel was a lot more comfortable than I thought, on straw-filled cushions. The camels are strange, the way they tuck their hind legs under, which does not look at all comfortable. Then we climbed a short ladder and perched ourselves on the bags, one camel for me and one for Lesley. As they stand up we were jostled back and forth, as they had two knees on their front legs and go up one at a time. They moaned and groaned but off we went.

We saw some succulent bushes, some flowering cacti and lots of sand and stones.

Our "camel boy" was named Salima, a jolly teenager.

We soon stopped at a place that, from a distance, looked like a palace, but close up we could see it was mausoleum, tombs of the family of a Maharaja.

Soon we stopped again at a water hole for lunch, chapati, vegetable subji, oranges and coffee in the shade of a tree, with those ultra-cheap tiny bidi cigarettes to smoke. Bidis are small hand-rolled tobacco in tendu or temburni leaf, an Indian plant. This place was called Barabagh.

Later as we continued into the desert, we came upon the ancient capital of Lodhruva, with a Jain Temple and a black-faced god with wings and large eyes, that had been rebuilt in the 1970's. There was a lot of camel and cow shit in the desert.

Rajasthan Desert Song

by
Alun Buffry

Lesley and I went down to Rajasthan
Desert, with Salima, a camel riding man.
Through a morning trotting on,
Just the sound of Salima's songs.
Peahens, crows and tinkle bells,
Crowds of men at water wells,
Telling tales of who-knows-what
While we're wishing it not so hot.
Stop for lunch, a shady tree,
Eat some vegetable chapati,
Drinking some chai, hot and sweet
Try to avoid the deadly heat.
All around us golden sand,
Shrubs and cacti about this land.
"Be careful please, where you sit,
"Cos desert's full of camel shit."

At about 6.30, we stopped for the evening for dinner at another water hole. Suddenly a wind came up, with moisture in it so we thought it was going to rain. But it didn't rain at all. We slept under a tree. I awoke during the night and wow, what a clear starry sky!

29th March

Up, breakfast and ready to go at some unearthly hour but it was overcast and cooler until about 10.30. We passed several small villages but saw no activity. There were wild camels in the distance. Our camels seemed to fart a lot.

When it became hotter, we stopped at the Sam sand dunes at a water hole for lunch. Salima invited me to follow him for a "very good site". I imagined a fantastic view over a valley with the walled city of Jaiselmer or somewhere equally exotic in the distance, as we winded in and out between the dunes. Suddenly, he stopped.

"Look," he smiled and smirked.

As I looked around, all I could see was sand. Not even my own footprints. I realised quickly that I was at his mercy. If he ran off I would maybe not find my way back. All I would be able to do was shout and hope that the others came and rescued me. I didn't even have my water bottle. I thought I would last long if he ran off.

Thankfully he didn't and just took me back. We weren't actually a long way from the others, maybe just the other side of a dune. The sand was very hot and rippled, and ran into my footprint as soon as I took another step. I should have spotted where the sun was, but so trusting I was.

We spent about 4 hours there before continuing for another hour before stopping for lime and soda in a small village; better than the warm, treated water we had in our bottles that was keeping us alive. The village had a small shop that sold a few vegetables, Coca Cola and Fanta and cigarettes, what everyone seemed to want even right out here in the desert.

The guide gave me a small lump of opium which I ate. That helped me relax. Another surprise. Who would have thought, eating opium with a camel in the desert!

Another beautifully clear starry night at another water hole.

30th March

That morning we started out at 7.30; it was already hot. We stopped at a deserted desert village called Culdrah which had quite a large temple. There were few images here, just some mutilated statues and a few poor ones of monkeys. Salima said, or rather agreed to what I had said, that people left due to lack of water. But later a Canadian guy we met on his own Safari trek said it was because there had been a lot of conflict driven by Moslem invaders from Pakistan against the Hindus about eleven years earlier (1974) .

By 10.30, it was so hot that I was falling asleep on the camel.

We spotted another couple of camels coming towards us and they waved us closer. One had a Japanese girl on top, red faced looking exhausted. Her camel-driver guide said she would not drink the water. I gave her some purifying tablets and told he she must drink – it was even sometimes better to drink dirty water than not to drink at all, but the water from the well was OK, which was why they call it well water. She left happier. Now I thought, maybe I saved her life.

Almost suddenly we were on our way back to Jaiselmer. We stopped at a small village called Amar Sagar where a Jain Temple was being restored.

Suddenly we spotted Jaiselmer in the distance.

JAISELMER

(Rajasthan, 1985)

by

Alun Buffry

Jaiselmer, oh Jaiselmer

Not a lot of hassle here.

Just cows walking in the streets,

Adding smells to earthly heat,

Makes us want to drink more chai,

But "No milk!" the people cry.

All those cows yet still no milk,

All those shops that just sell silk,

Desert life's just not the same,

Camels struggling, what a shame,

To let us climb upon their backs

And if they moan they know the crack.

Driver up there perched on top

Passing songs until we stop

At water hole or shady tree

To eat a precious chapati

Made by the men, full of pride,

Over fires with veggies fried,

In spices which do not have names,

But we don't care 'cos we have pains,

In legs and arms and even feet

From riding camels in this heat.

Three days the desert journeyed on,

We listened to the Rajput's songs,

Passing temples, villages

Passed to us through ages.

Suddenly, the words we hear:

"See over there, sweet Jaiselmer!"

Back in the Hotel Fort View. All in all it was sometimes a bit too hot but it was an incredible experience although Lesley said that her coccyx was struggling and she still says she never recovered (now in 2021). She was also upset because she'd lost a bead from her hair.

The hotel manager asked me to write a comment in his guest book, which I did. I read through some of the other comments which were all positive. One read: "The best thing about riding the camels is that one could fart loudly and blame it on the camels."

3ʳ1st March

Jaiselmer was built in 1156 on Trikuta Hillby Rawal Jaisal – did I already write that?

There are 99 bastions around the circumference. It was very impressive. Just inside was a seven story palace and Jain temples from the twelfth to fifteenth centuries, dedicated to Rikhabdeuti and Sambhavantiji. The temples are only open until 11 AM. Also there was a Shiva Temple and Ganesh Temple. Ganesh is the elephant-headed god.

We spent most of the rest of the day in the hotel, just wandering out for a delicious lemon lassi drink and a 'special' cheese toast sandwich with garlic, onion and tomato. We tried to buy some henna for Lesley, without success. We saw a monkey sitting on a wall, eating a tomato, and lots of cows wandering about the streets.

Wherever we go in India, once we stop, we see people looking at us with no sense of embarrassment.

EYES

by

Alun Buffry

In India, no matter where,

The people seem to stand and stare,

Looking mostly at Lesley,

Her wondrous form just there to see.

As if she's wondering around topless,

Ignoring all the smelly mess.

But then it's India here we're told,

Their staring seems to be quite bold.

They don't realise she gets upset

She's not quite used to it quite yet.

Women, men and children look,

As if we're out of some special book,

But maybe she'd take it more pleasantly,

If they had used some subtlety.

1st April.

They had April Fools Day here, but no tricks.

We visited some mansions built by the rich traders that passed through on the trade route before Bombay was opened up as a major port. Patwon Ki was the best; outside was intricate stone carvings and lattices; inside paintings. Another was Salim Singh, about 300 years old. That one had been lived in by a prime minister called Salim Singh, who built two storeys of wood on top, but that was later torn down by Maharaja.

Our next stop was a shop where I bought beautiful silk paintings and more cotton dresses.

Whilst we were inside the shop, all of a sudden there was a downpour of very heavy rain, apparently the first time in years, with rushing water washing down the streets for about an hour.

This was our last night here and we are both sad to have to

leave.

2nd April

We arrived in Jodhpur at 6,30 AM. We soon met a guy who said he was a doctor and a young guy Ramesh who collected stamps. The doctor said he could change our ticket to a second class on a super-fast train back to Delhi. It seemed like a good idea but Ramesh warned us against it. We went to the ticket office where another chap warned us, saying we would not get a refund until back in Delhi and maybe not even then. So we kept our tickets for the train at 15.10.

When we took breakfast it was already 10.30. We ordered cornflakes, toast and jam with coffee. But when it arrived it was tea, so we asked for coffee. It came back in the same teapot. We were sure they had just added coffee to the tea! Soon we were back down Agra Street for spicy samosa and superb thick lemon lassi. Then we had poached eggs and chips.

It was soon time to board the train and the doctor turned up to say goodbye and for some reason gave us his son's address in Delhi.

3rd April: Delhi Again

We arrived back in Delhi early morning. The train was very slow for a good few miles before pulling into the station. From the carriage window it was a real sight for sore eyes. We were moving alongside a shanty town and the large number of people there clearly had few facilities and were using the railway track as a public convenience; there was a long line of bare arses facing us. I could only imagine the excrement dried up every day or maybe was eaten by rats. Not a pleasant sight or thought but then again, quite funny.

Also on the journey some of our fellow passengers somehow got the idea that I could read palms. One guy gave me a piece of paper to write on; I saw it was an invitation for a job interview so told him he was about to get a new job. He seemed very pleased and I hope it encouraged him so he got the job. But that only encouraged others. I just made some positive stuff up telling them all good news or good changes were coming. Indians are a very superstitious nation.

That day, as it turned out, was the holiday day for Lord Mahavir Jayanti, although most shops were open. So after getting back to the Ashok Yatri Newas hotel and checking in, we planned to get some passport photos done in preparation for our applications for visas to Nepal.

Two people were arguing at reception because they were told they had to pay in foreign currency like pounds or dollars. For us this was to be a nuisance too, as previously they had taken rupees with an exchange chit. So now Lesley had to change a travellers check into rupees, then change enough for the hotel bills back into pounds. In India there were ever changing rules and regulations, a bureaucratic system that wanted everything in triplicate.

By now all my white shirts were either stained and dirty, so we had to get them cleaned too. It would have been cheaper to buy new shirts.

We went back to the office to see Ali and get details for our trip to Nepal and find out about visas. There was another guy there. He said "Ah, I see you have been in the desert, because you have a red nose! I have been too, you see I have a white nose!" He explained that though my nose was burned red, his was bleached white!

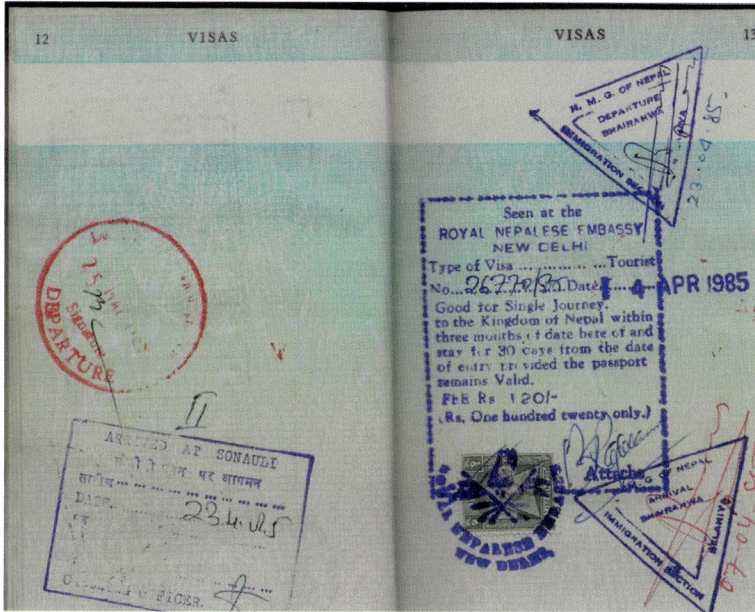

4th April

The visa for Nepal cost 120 rupees each, about six pounds. That was no problem for us. Ali sent somebody to get our passports stamped.

Apparently, Delhi had 50,000 rickshaws, one million bicycles, 3000 animal-drawn carts and 80.000 motor vehicles including cars, buses, trucks and rickshaws, resulting in 5000 road accidents every year.

That day we strolled along Parliament Street and Janpath area trying to find Jantar Mantar astronomical gardens and observatory, which was supposed to be just a short walk from Connaught Circus. After quite a long walk up the wrong street, we came across a Sikh Temple. Suddenly we were back on Ashok Road at our hotel.

© Sahil Ahuja

We had missed Jantar Mantar altogether!

Then we learned that Parliament Street was actually called Sansad Marg, which we had passed several times whilst walking back and forth. By then we had learned that Jantar Mantar was just behind our hotel, on the "backside" as they say here. So off we went again.

Jantar Mantar was a collection of stone astronomical instruments built by Maharaja Jai Singh The Second about 1725. There was a large salmon-coloured odd shaped structure with steps everywhere, a huge sun dial supposed to be accurate to half a second and another triangular shape and semicircles meant for plotting the courses of the stars and predicting eclipses and predict the times and movements of the sun, moon and planets.

It was difficult to see how they were used but it included the use of shadows cast upon graduated concave plates. It was all set in a green garden patch.   The word Jantar was derived from yantra, meaning instrument, while the suffix Mantar was derived from mantrana meaning consult or calculate.

6th April

So we booked out of the Ashok Yatri Newas hotel. We had to get a special slip from reception to present to the security guard on the door. This took ten minutes. When we got to the door, the guard wasn't there.

Next we took a rickshaw down to the Tourist Camp to board the "Deluxe India super coach" which looks like a wreck, to Kathmandu. The 4 PM departure time became 4.45, not too bad for India. At about 11 PM that night, the coach broke down.

After very little sleep it was 8 AM and the coach had not moved.

PRAYING FOR A BUS

by

Alun Buffry

We left Delhi 4 P.M. today
To Kathmandu by bus
But midnight whilst still on the way
We stopped without a fuss.

It had been quite a bumpy ride
Through places without names

The seating wasn't very wide
No sleep, it was a shame.

Half day upon this bus we are
Frying in the heat,
This is no deluxe bus by far
It is a lying cheat.

Another bus soon coming here,
Well that is what we're told,
Exactly when is not made clear,
No Indian is that bold.

Then still we're waiting on the bus,
Later on that day,
A Foreign girl invited us
To come along and pray.

"We'll do some prayers and puja chants
And maybe sing a song,
If that don't work we'll maybe dance
And bus will come along."

The bus to Kathmandu we think

Will much improve our mood,

And on the way, perhaps a drink,

And then a plate of food.

"Oh bus! Oh bus! Show us your magic!

Come and save this day,

For this trip we're on is become quite tragic..."

Oh! Now we're on our way!

7ᵗʰ April

I felt as if we'd worked out some bad Karma after such a bumpy ride, being at the back of the bus and constantly being tossed into the air, often hitting my head on the inside bus roof and hardly sleeping at all.

We reached the border with Nepal about 10 AM. We were still here at 5.30.

The Nepalese customs officers seemed to be looking through every Nepalese and Indians cases and bags, but not ours.

This place was called Sunauli. It was very dry and dusty. We had a good Thali meal for lunch; that's a metal plate with small amounts of vegetable, rice, potatoes, yoghurt, chapati. It cost next to nothing.

We had now been approached by a group of boys and young teenagers; they were very friendly and seemed to think that Lesley was a film star. They provided us with information and directed us to a bank. One boy, named Sankara, just wanted his photo taken with Lesley. I did not want to get the camera out.

There were a number of younger kids about, trying get us to change money or to sell us cold drinks or spicy cucumber slices; cucumber was one of the few fruits or vegetables that I detest.

The journey from the border was again very bumpy. In the future I will offer baksheesh if necessary for a seat up front. We stopped along the road at a couple of nameless places for chai. In one place there were jugs of water on the tables. They had bits floating in. I saw an old guy remove his scarf and use it as a filter.

Eventually we arrived in Kathmandu and were taken by bicycle rickshaw to our hotel. It's about £5 a night for a double.

8th April: Kathmandu

The hotel and room are clean and we had a hot shower and room service. At 7 AM the view from the window facing westerly was magic, with several pagodas and stretching over the city to the distant mountains, with a very magical palace-looking building on the hill. The light was perfect.

At dawn the city wakes to the sounds of chanting and singing, bells and musical instruments, car horns and beeps.

Later though, it became hazy.

WAKING IN NEPAL

by

Alun Buffry

Outside

Is a cloudy sky, bright sun between, a slight breeze,

The sound of one man chanting.

And all elsewhere a few notes on some type of magic flute -

A strange cacophony of bells and horns and clattering.

No two horns seem to sound the same.

Another engine? Sounds like a tractor - probably a bus!

Beep, beep, beep.

If I look out of the window I see tin rooftops,

Blimsen Tower, a glorious white standing before the blue;

And there - a temple, a pagoda, a woman sitting with washing lay out to dry,

Pigeons coo-ing, crows a-crowing, gardens growing,

Potted plants that people tend,

A bicycle rickshaw, a cow, a man with a bundle of wood on his head!

A cockerel crows as another motorbike passes 3 men trying to move a fridge,

Young girl, proud, staring into space,

Three boys rolling rubber wheels of glee amidst the rubble,

Whilst more look on admiringly.

Yet another dog - a tempo (three-wheeler) barking as two boys, hand-in-hand,

Laugh at a goat.

Cock crows, horns, far away mountainous silences

Surround the Monkey Temple,

Like a golden palace on the hill.

Behind - another hill.

Shame about the dusty haze.

We spent most of the day resting up, sitting on a hotel balcony recovering from that dreadful journey, but it's feeling very good here. I reckoned we'd try to get some Nepalese hash tomorrow. We had spaghetti, rice pudding and a sad looking scone for dinner followed by an early night.

9th April

I slept to the sound of barking dogs and awoke feeling exhausted and not too well.

Again we heard devotional songs, chanting and bells. We had to sort out tickets back to Delhi for a couple of weeks time and get a city map, then go exploring.

It was not at all like I had imagined it, not really like India at all. There was a lot of British stuff in the shops; cigarettes and rolling tobacco and skins, chocolates and sweets and alcohol, all cheap.

Nepal was a religiously tolerant country, with Buddhists, Hindus, Muslims, Christians and other all living together seemingly in mutual respect and tolerance. Restaurants sell meat and fish meals as well as plenty of vegetarian.

We strolled about the Square and found Freak Street, where all the westerners, Americans and Australians go, famous for its hash shops. Ganga Road and the Post Office.

I bought some cheap headphones, then we went back to Durbar Square.

There was a collection of many temples there. As we walked, we saw the Shiva-Pavati Temple and from a window there people watching the street below. Some temples had erotic carvings of Tantric yoga, in particular the Jagnarth Temple. Some people believe that the carvings were done in praise of the goddess of lightning, whom, being a chaste virgin, would not strike a temple with such shocking carvings.

Behind that temple we saw the Kalo Bhairab, a massive stone image of the said-to-be terrifying Black Bharab. This was once used as a lie detector; suspected wrongdoers were forced to touch the feet of the god and swear innocence and anyone that told untruths would die.

The Palace was near here. Along the outside there are inscriptions in eighteen languages including English and French. It was established by King Malla in the seventeenth century. Legend says that milk will flow from the spout in the middle if anyone can read all the languages.

At the gate to the palace was a statue of Hanuman, the monkey-headed devotee of Rama. His face was obscured by red paint put on it by the faithful.

There was a police station on one side of the square and near here there are giant drums built in the eighteenth century.

Also near here lies the Kumari Devi Temple. This was three storeys high.

There was also another temple here, the Taleju Temple, dedicated to a family deity and built in the sixteenth century.

At 115 feet in height, it was Durbar Square's most magnificent temple stands at its north-eastern extremity but was not open to the public. Even for Hindus, admission was restricted; they can only visit it briefly during the annual Dasain festival. The 35m-high temple was built in 1564 by Mahendra Malla. Taleju Bhawani was originally a goddess from the south of India, but she became the titular deity, or royal goddess, of the Malla kings in the 14th century. The temple stands on a 12-stage plinth, dominating the Durbar Sq area. The eighth stage of the plinth forms a wall around the temple, in front of which are 12 miniature temples. Four more miniature temples stand inside the wall, which had four beautifully carved wide gates.

When we left the Square, we bought some reasonable but not excellent quality hash near the Swiss Travellers Restaurant and ate an excellent fish tandoori just down the road in the Other Room and Bar. Lesley had paratha and salad and we washed it down with brandy coffee – all for about six UK pounds.

It seemed like there are a few interesting places worth seeing not far from Kathmandu. A bus ride to Bhaktapur and a short trek to be considered.

10th April

It rained during the night. That had freshened the air.

We walked to the Post Office again and then went to Bhimsem Tower also called Dharahara. This was a nine-storey, 203 foot tower at the centre of Sundhara. It was built in 1832 by Mukhtiyar, equivalent to a prime minister, under the commission of Gueen Lalit Tripurasundari. The tower had a spiral staircase containing 213 steps. The eighth floor had a circular balcony for observers that provided a panoramic view of the valley.

Then we went to near the park to see where the buses to Patan leave from.

So then we went to Tina Travel to confirm the bus back to Delhi on the 23rd. Nothing being as simple as we thought, we were told that he would need to contact Ali to change the dates for our trip to Kashmir, so we had a few more days here. We also booked bus tickets to Pokhara. The money we have was going fast but that could not be helped. I decide to write back to Norwich for more money and get it sent to Delhi or Kashmir.

KATMANDONEIN
by
Alun Buffry

Now we've been in Kathmandu a while.
Is it just the highness makes us smile?
Is it the atmosphere makes us light?
Or the mountains within our sight?

Lesley reckons people here take bigger steps!

120

Maybe they are all secret tantric cult adepts?
Anyway you look at it, they're happy
Even if their ways are sometimes crappy!

How come everything here seems so cheap?
Yet money seems so hard to keep?
Don't seem to spend a lot in any place
Just drifting round the city in a space.

Decided to stay here a few more days,
Smoking trying not to get out-hazed.
In the morning here if there is no sun,
Read a local Tantric yoga book, it could be fun.

11th April

We went to bed early last night, before 10, and woke up at 6.30 feeling tired. I didn't think I had fully recovered from the bus ride from Delhi and maybe a bit dehydrated. Also I was becoming more irritated by flies.

But there was plenty of lovely bird song to lift the mood. As we looked down from our window we saw a small courtyard with what looks like a shrine with a small lingam, opposite the hotel. I had not noticed that before. But it was no big surprise as there were shrines everywhere, many seemingly abandoned and uncared for.

The eyes we saw that are painted on some temples and other places were the all-seeing eyes of Lord Buddha, often incorporated into statues of Hindu gods in Nepal and seen as an incarnation of Vishnu, as were Rama and Krishna. There are quite a few temples and statues of Ganeesh, the elephant-headed god.

Ganeesh was not actually an elephant, but an elephant-headed humanoid, also known as Ganesha Ganapati and Vinayaka, and was one of the best-known and most worshipped deities in the Hindu Pantheon. He was widely revered as the remover of obstacles; the patron of arts and sciences; and the diva of intellect and wisdom. As the god of beginnings, he was honoured at the start of rites and ceremonies. Ganesha was also invoked as patron of letters and learning during writing sessions.

Ganesha was the son of Shiva and Parvati and he was the brother of Karthikeya (or Subrahmanya), the god of war. He was created by his mother using earth which she moulded into the shape of a boy. As Shiva was away on his meditative wanderings, Parvati set her new son as guard while she bathed. Unexpectedly, Shiva returned home and, on finding the boy, and outraged at his impudence in claiming he was Parvati's son, Shiva called for his gang of demons, the bhutaganas, who fought ferociously with the boy. However, the youngster easily held his own against such fearsome adversaries and Vishnu was forced to intervene in the form of Maya and, whilst the boy was distracted by her beauty, the demons, or Shiva himself, lopped off his head. At the commotion, Parvati ran from her bath and remonstrated with Shiva for so summarily killing their son. Repentant, Shiva ordered a new head to be found for the boy and, as the first animal available was an elephant, so Ganesha gained a new head and became the most distinctive of the Hindu gods.

That day we took a three-wheeler tempo to Patan, which cost us about 50 pence.

Patan, sometimes called Lalitpur, was on the other side of the Bagmati river; the name means City of Beauty. It was the second city in the Kathmandu valley, but nowadays it's really just part of Kathmandu itself. It's a Buddhist place. We get out of the tempo just outside the city gate, where we find the Royal cafe and stop for a samosa. Then we walk down some very smelly streets with open sewage and rubbish, to reach another square. On the way we visit a Buddhist monastery called Hiranya Varna Mahabihar, built in the twelfth century with its gold-plated roofs. Inside we see many prayer wheels and paintings of Buddha. It was a three-storey structure with Buddha images in the courtyard.

Nearby was the five-storey Shiva Temple called Kumbeshwar; the water in the courtyard was supposed to come from Gosain Kunda, a lake in Nepal's national park at over 14,000 feet. It was considered as the abode of the Hindu deities Shiva and Gauri.

Patan's Durbar Square was crowded with temples. The first seen in Bhimsen Temple with a pillar at the front and a lion on top. Bhimsen was a character from the scripture called the Mahabharata and one of the strongest people that ever lived.

Next to the shiva temple are two stone elephants that guard the door.

Also in the Square are two statues, one of King Malla on the other of Narasimha, and another Shiva temple.

Down one side of the square was the Sundari Chow or beautiful yard.

There we saw the royal bath and a small replica of the Krishna Temple. Inside the courtyard there were three statues of the gods Ganga and Jumna, standing or dancing on a crocodile and turtle.

Back outside in the street, we saw statues of Ganeesh, Narsimha and Hanuman.

12th April

We were told that it was now Nepalese New Years Eve. We did not walk far, feeling a bit queasy, maybe due to altitude.

Looking for New Year

by

Alun Buffry

Kathmandu: morning mist, disappears, mountain view...
Clouds spreading, sun shines, sky turns seamless blue.
Magic palace on the hill, silver morning light,
As the haze clears away, giving city sights.

Street below slowly wakes, dogs with horns and bells
All the homeless people there, washing at the wells.
Today is Nepalese New Year, should be celebrations,
Where they are is not too clear, to our mild frustration.

Maybe dancing in the street, or are there parades?
No-one here seems able to tell, where New Year's Day is made.
Life goes on as usual, everywhere you glance,
New Year doesn't seem like here, the spirit to enhance.

Where would we go in England,

If New Year we were there?

Down a pub or round a house

Or down Trafalgar Square?

I guess that from outside, it'd look all much the same,

Like we don't celebrate New Year, they'd think it was a shame.

So maybe here in Nepal, because I cannot see,

There's celebrations all around, invisible to me.

13th April

It was New Years Day in Nepal.

The Sikh guy, Navneet Singh, who we met at the hotel roof last night, let us use his taxi for free, so we visited Daxinkali, about a 45 minute drive away.

The drive there had some great views through the Chobar Gorge. Legend says that the valley was once a lake and once the god Manjushree, the god of wisdom, struck a rock with his sword and water came out, sweeping away all the snakes. But the snake king, Karkotak, who lived here was now in a nearby pond called Taudaha Balaju, in a small park with flowers and ponds with black fish and water spouts.

Inside was also the small image of a Sleeping Vishnu which the King of Nepal was allowed to see whenever he wants, and a small temple flanked by Hindu temples dedicated to Ganeesh and Buddha, with a Shiva lingam

Here was the temple to the goddess Kali and every Saturday,

like this day, there was a scene of the devotional slaughter of goats and chickens, with pools of blood; they are killed in the temple and washed in the dirty water outside, then taken for a feast. There was a long line of people queuing to kill.

There was a larger Sleeping Vishnu at Budhanilkantha, where he was laying on a bed of snakes. It was said he sleeps for four months each year, separating the monsoon season. Legend said that a farmer, whilst tilling his land, struck the stone below and blood came out. Every morning there was prayer and devotional rituals involving rice, vegetables and money and even a bottle of sauce. The King of Nepal himself was said to be an incarnation of Shiva and not allowed to see this place. Strangely it felt like Holy ground, more than any of the other temples.

By 1 PM we were back in Kathmandu eating egg and chips.

We found out that the palace on the hill was actually a Buddhist temple at Swayambhunath; it was also called the Monkey Temple.

14th April

We lazed in bed until midday, chatting and smoking. By the time we reached Eat at Joe's for banana and honey pancakes with lassi drink and lemon tea, it was already very hot. It's more humid here than Delhi. I am not happy with the quality of the hash we bought yesterday so I took it back. I managed to swap it but that was no good either. The guy said they only sell weak stuff because otherwise "hippies sit in the street and that is bad". So I asked for my money back and he gave it to me.

Late afternoon, we walked round Durbar Square, down the streets and bazaars called Indrachowk and Kel Tole. On the way back we found Pig Alley or Pie Alley and a nice cafe with excellent lemon meringue pie and walnut custard pie. That evening I had Prawn with peas and cashew nuts at Ani Anis restaurant with beer. I must say there was a much greater variety of food here than in India where we had been. There were extensive India, Chinese, Italian and other menus as well as Nepalese food.

15th April: Pokhara

We got up at 5 AM to catch the 6.30 bus to Pokhara. It was a pleasant journey with beautiful scenery and often children on the side of the road. We passed four rivers, the Trishuli, the Marshyangdi and the Seti Gandaki, then a bridge over the Madi.

We passed many paddy fields. At Mugling, a small town, we saw the longest suspension bridge in Nepal over the Trishuli

river. It looked like a lovely little town.

Pokhara itself seemed a quiet peaceful place. We stayed at the Ashok Guest House, with a great small garden, restaurant and beautiful view of the mountains. It cost us £2 a night for a double.

The lake was called Phewa.

In the afternoon we walked to the end of the village, along several roads, both tarmac and rubble, to rows of supply shops for trekkers, restaurants, cheap lodges and souvenir shops. We passed the Royal Palace but it did not look like there was much to see. We passed a small temple with a walled garden full of marijuana plants, more rows of stalls, passed the Guru Restaurant and the Anand Restaurant, then sat by the lake under a tree.

The only unpleasant things here were the flies and the young hasslers; the latter, at least, seemed to be doing well out of tourists, all shouting Namaste and trying to put a distance between us and what little money we had to spare.

17th April

We decided to going to laze around that day. When we went into the garden we saw that the cloudy haze had cleared and behind the mountains we had seen were massive snow- packed peaks, the Fishtail Mountain, Machapuchare.

But we were both feeling short of energy and did not want to do much but we had some good grass to help us relax.

As the Mind flies so the Bird walks to the mountain, OR Zen and the Art of Being Lazy

(a postcard from Kathmandu)

by Alun Buffry

Today, outside, the weather is hazy.

Stayed in all day, feeling quite lazy.

Where to go now, we often talk,

Then decide it's too far to walk.

Two hours there and two hours back,

"Let's stay here, and have a snack".

Just fifteen minutes up to Baba's.

And we know that there, food's better by far,

But here we eat, for our stomachs sake,

Whatever's available as it's no effort to make.

"Well", I say, "I guess that's what

A holiday's for on a day that's hot."

"We're free, we don't have to do anything.

We can fly like a bird with a broken wing."

"How can that be, such a bird can't fly?"

"We can't do much either and here is why-

Cos - cor it's hot outside today,

And wherever we go we have to pay",

Or "My leg's aching, stiff and weak,

And there's nothing in the bazaar we seek."

"Stomach queasy, or head aching?

Let's be another chillum a-making."

Then, "Let's go in a boat!"

"No, don't want to row!"

Or, "Let's climb that mountain, look at the snow!"

Oh, if only we could get up there and back,

Without having to walk on that mountain track.

If you close your eyes and lay on your bed,

You can go anywhere inside your head.

If you know how to master the Traveller's Trick,

You'll be there in an instant and come back so quick.

But later we did go to see the "Cultural After Sunset Dancing" at the Hotel Fishtail Lodge near the lake, original Nepalese dancing troupe. We went across the lake on a wooden raft pulled by a yellow rope. An hour of dancing plus transport cost us £6 each but beers were £8. It was fun anyway and afterwards we went to Baba's eating house for grilled fish and chips.

Annapurna For Sale

The calm serenity of Annapurna
Sweeps lazily over the town Pokhara;
People here have more time to smile,
Occasionally to come chat a while.

"Namaste, hello, good morning" they say
Then to business or change money.
Still, at least themselves they try to keep,
Yet their starting price is steep
"American, French, where you from?"
Like the opening line of a Nepalese song,
Which they teach in their local schools,
To say to tourists who like fools,
Are parted from their cash to soon,
As "Better prices before afternoon,
Or "First business I make today with you,
"So if you like one, why not buy two?"
Whether beggars or hasslers or honest men,
Want dollars, pounds or even yen.
As much as mountains beautiful
We all need a living our stomachs to fill.
"Here we are, no problem way of life,
"Is she your friend or is she wife?
"You want charas or marid-u-are-na,
"Opium, mushroom or brown sugar?"
"What you want buy?", so often heard,
As if just looking is absurd.
It would be good to walk one day,
Without these offers filling our way,
To absorb life's energy so obviously close,
But then that's part of it, I suppose.

18ᵗʰ April

We did nothing that day but eat, smoke and relax.

19th April

This day we took a shaky meccano-like bus to another Post Office near Mahandra Pool and started to walk to the bazaar but it was of no interest to us so we took the bus back to the lakeside and had lunch, vegetable dopiaza for me and buffalo cutlet for Lesley, at the Hotel Snowland. We scored some weed on the way back to our hotel. Thunder just as we arrived. There was no clear view of the Annapurna mountain range or the Fishtail. There were no bicycle rickshaws in Pokhara.

20th April

That day we took the bus back to Kathmandu; we both enjoyed Pokhara and would like to come back here one day, but that happens to many places that I visit, especially after leaving!

The bus seemed quite cramped at times but we had some great views again.

137

So we arrived back at the Hotel Eden, where we stayed before. We had a problem with the taps that were hard to turn and the toilet would not flush so we had to pour down water from a bucket from the bath. The bath had no plug. The radio had only one station.

We were in a different room, now with a view of Bhimsen tower in all its glory.

21st April

A horrible day, we both felt dreadful and just wanted to sleep all day. Maybe it was the altitude. It was 4600 feet above sea level, about the same as Ben Nevis. We did manage to get down to Freak Street to the Magic Apple, for dinner of sweet and sour chicken.

Lesley dropped the lid off the cistern trying to get it to flush and it broke on the floor. This room was not as good as the other one. It had holes in the windows! Opposite us was a room with some noisy and dodgy-looking guys, so all in all, we were both feeling irritated. We were also fed up with street hasslers trying to change money or sell drugs including heroin.

The national newspaper here in English was The Rising Nepal. It was six sides of news from around the world including news of dawn raids by the Indian Army at he Golden Temple in Amritsar, a very beautiful place that I visited and stayed at in

1972. Also explosions in Brussels and other pieces about Ronald Regan, lepers in Nepal and quotes from King Birenda (Benda) telling people to do well. Also people had been arrested for drugs in Pokhara. There was also a shortage of drinking water in Pokhara, a facelift had been ordered for the Krishna Temple in Durbar Square. A Dutchman at the airport had been arrested with two kilos of hashish. The world went on while we were away, far from most of it but then still close.

22nd April

Still felt weak. We had breakfast at a place called Mom's, muesli, mango juice and tea. Then we wandered up to the nearby supermarket which was in reality a row of shops and a three-storey building with more shops. So back in the hotel still feeling bad but a cup of chai and a chillum helped.

The Sikh guy Mavneet Singh reappeared at the hotel. He said he was back to continue his gambling investments at a casino, this time for a week. He never seemed to smile, even though he was quite pleasant and friendly.

We were offered some good quality jump suits made from cotton and Lesley asked if they could be altered to include a zip and a pocket. We ordered about a dozen, they were very cheap, so Lesley went off to collect them and she was well pleased. I will sell them back in Norwich.

I had been reading Paul Scott's book, 'Staying On', which I had just finished.

It was a good read. He builds up Tusker to a character we feel we know and then we lose him when he dies and his wife suffers with sadness and fright at being alone in India, until the end which comes as a shock, but hammers home the common situations people can fall into. All after a lifetime togetherness even with all the personal differences and likes and dislikes, fondness and hatred, fears and passions for one's partner; suddenly one must be terribly alone. Alone, we seem to me to be constantly trying to build bridges, to dream that we can reach a common knowledge and awareness of each other so we are not alone like the islands that they say we may be. We so often want to be a part of somebody else, intermingled, so our differences can be overlooked, whether that was good or bad, each to see oneself in the other. That can be and usually was hard work but if tackled bravely and with passion, can be rewarding, for a while. Be alone but be not afraid to be with others. Til death us do part.

23rd April

We were up at 5 AM ready for the bus back to Delhi, but a problem getting breakfast or a taxi from the Hotel Eden after we ordered both last night. Eventually we got to the Hotel Withies to board the bus.

This time we had good front seats.

The journey down the valley was smooth with some good scenery, although the driver seemed to think he was on a race track. Nobody on the road seemed to want to get out of anyone else's way. The rule here was simple: "Might is Right".

It now seemed that many Nepalese and Indians like playing head games, so when when we said chai, char, tea, we were met with blank stares. Then, if you shouted, like barking an order, they suddenly understood. Maybe they were all just stoned.

We reached the border with no problem and the customs came and took all our passports to inspect whilst we sat on the bus outside the customs shed. They did not inspect any luggage.

But whilst we sat there a young boy outside spotted Lesley through the window. He obviously recognised her from when we passed through before. He was knocking on and waving through the window. Lesley waved back. He ran off and soon returned with some other boys and motioned us to open the window. They started throwing newspaper packages through the window. I opened one. It was weed. We are right outside the customs office. I through it back out shaking my head. More came in. I through them back shouting no. A couple of minutes later a guy came from further back on the bus and gave me two wraps, saying that the boys had asked him to give them to me. I threw them out too.

After a while the boys waved goodbye and left and soon we were on our way. The last thing I wanted was to get busted for weed at the border.

Across from us were two guys, one looked like David Soul from the Miami Vice TV series. They were smoking small joints and passed one to me. There was just enough for Lesley and I to have two puffs each. It was wonderful and strong Nepalese hash. They said they had trekked into the mountains to a village to get it. They made another small joint and we had another puff.

The bus took off and we were flying several feet high.

Into the darkness we went.

A few hours down the road, the bus suddenly stopped. It was the Indian customs officers.

They came on the bus and immediately told me to get off the bus. Strangely, as I was holding my shoulder bag on my lap, I passed it to Lesley. They ignored that. They also ignored Starksy and Hutch. They got some people from the back of the bus too, Nepalese I think.

It was dark outside so they all had torches, about six cops. They took me to the back boot and got me to show them my rucksack, which I opened and they emptied. They took my camera, a torch (the bulb no longer worked) and a tin a sardines. I told them the camera was cheap and so I did not need to declare it, the torch bulb was no good and the tin was fish. One guy said that if the fish were inside, they would be dead. Then another guy, presumably their boss, came and said "OK, mister, what you have?" I told him camera, torch and fish. He said "Is that all?" I said yes and he said "OK, get back on bus."

That was the end of that. They searched some other bags and off we went again, to Delhi.

24th April: Back in Delhi Yet Again

By 9 AM it was very very hot on the bus. We were both aching, queasy and probably dehydrated.

We passed through a place called Bareilly. There was a modern looking place with some nice architecture. Suddenly, a little further on, we realised this was the dump of place where our other bus had broken down, on our way to Kathmandu. So that time we had sat there for many hours in the heat with just a tiny chai shack and our prayers and mosquitoes, whilst five minutes walk away was that lovely looking new place that probably had a restaurant.

Later we passed though Rampur, which was mentioned in the book 'Staying On'.

When we reached Delhi at about 6.30 PM. As we were getting off the coach, I looked under the seat to make sure we had not dropped anything. I found two newspaper wraps of weed, about ten grams or so. A nice surprise.

We took a rickshaw back to our regular hotel, Ashok Yatri Newas.

25th April

After breakfast we went to see Ali Baktoo at his office. There was no money from the UK for us. I felt let down by my lodger, Fat Stan. He owed me money and should have sent it by now.

It was 96 degrees Fahrenheit, 35.5 degrees Centigrade. We checked for mail at the post office and American Express, nothing.

There was a scooter strike that day. We walked to The Indian Coffeehouse in Connaught Circus area, which I had often visited in 1972.

Then we went back in the hotel to eat Masala Dosa and ice cream and felt better.

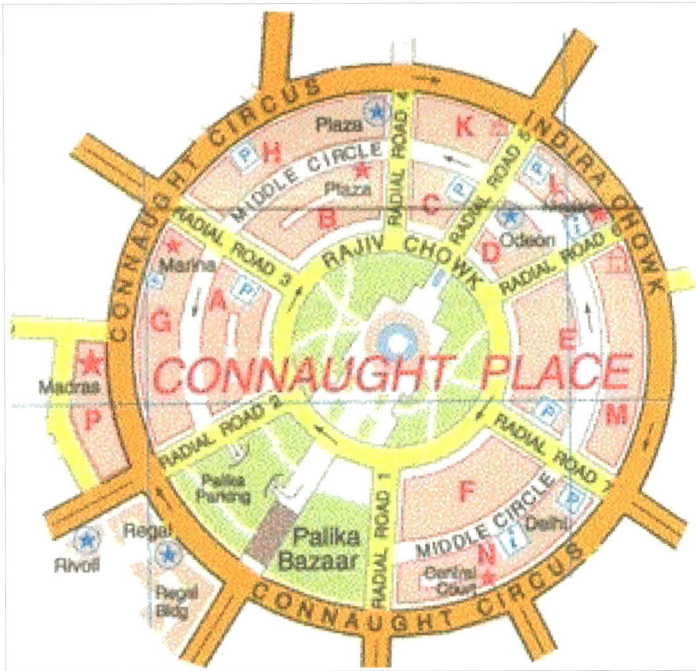

29[h] April: Kashmir by bus.

RAM RAM BUSES
by
Alun Buffry

From Delhi on an Indian Tourist bus,
We left thinking they'd take care of us.
An Indian video humbly plays and we're
Told in 24 hours we'll reach Kashmir.
The journey goes into the darkest night,
As jungle and hills slowly dodge our sight,
The road now is just long and straight,
No bumps and bends or jerks to hate.
We're speeding along, ever so fast,
As if this journey is our last,
The road the driver's trying to keep,
Me - I'm just trying to fall asleep.
Suddenly, we swerve, a crash, a jolt,
Us thrown around, bus comes to a halt,
We look through windows only to see,
We hit a small tractor and just missed a tree!
Spite driver's brave efforts to curve and sway,
One side of the bus has been torn right away!
Amidst cries of Oh God!" - in Hindi "Ram Ram",
And in my own mind "Oh shit, oh damn!"

No one here seems able to tell,

Whether we're earthly or in heaven or hell.

But nobody's hurt, so we all get out,

A policeman a sweeper's given a clout.

For without thought he's just learned that he'd officially signed

A statement unread because he was blind.

There's nothing to do now but sit and wait,

Arriving Kashmir we know we'll be late.

Then mosquitoes surround us and all rush in,

"There's three dozen humans in a half open tin!"

They must have shouted and told their friends,

"We can buzz all about them and insanity send!"

Well I know it's our blood they are trying to drink,

And "Kill the bastards" is what I think,

And now the sun has gotten bright,

People are gathering to smile at our site.

Apparently the tractor driver was drunk,

The cop wanted baksheesh or he'd be sunk.

Ah, now they're trying the bus to fix

With hammers, wires and broken sticks!

It'll be midnight tomorrow before we arrive,

If just 36 hours more we can somehow survive.

But surprise, surprise we weren't there all day,

For two hours later we were on our way.

30th April

We stayed the night at the Hotel Palace in Jammu, although not exactly a palace. We had to share a room with a Canadian guy. We were up at 6 AM to continue our journey on the bus.

Of course we were going to be many hours later so whoever was going to meet us at the bus depot will probably not be there.

It seemed to be that every long bus ride in India comes with a little adventure.

It was a nerve-wrecking drive through excellent scenery with sights such as monkeys and herds of goats along the way; sometimes we had to stop for the goats on the road. The herds and goats were driven along by what looks like whole families.

There was a 5200 foot long tunnel and signs reading "This is not a race or rally, this is Kashmir Valley". I was not sure that our driver could read though.

One surprise was seeing stalls along the way, selling cricket bats, made from local walnut.

Srinagar

When we finally arrived in Srinagar at about 6.30 PM, we were met by a group of young hasslers each claiming that they had been sent to meet us, not one seem to know of the name of the person that sent them, so we went to the office to phone Kashmir Himalayan Holidays. Before we got an answer, a guy arrived with all our details and off we go by Rickshaw and Shikara to our houseboat, the New Wild Rose.

Shikaras are of various sizes and are used for multiple purposes, including transportation.

The usual shikara seats six people, with the driver paddling at the rear. Like the Venetian gondolas. They are a cultural symbol of Kashmir. Some shikaras are still used for fishing, harvesting aquatic vegetation (usually for fodder), and transport, while most are covered with tarpaulins and are used by tourists.

We met Ibram and Bashir who were there supposedly to do our will. Omelette and chips served, we were shown to our room which was OK, but not as good as the Kashmir Paradise that I stayed in last November.

1ˢᵗ May

It rained all last night and most of the day, which I spent playing backgammon. It was almost chilly after Delhi. I was glad I had my sweater. Outside were some salesmen on their shikaras, touting for business. One was selling furs. Lesley had ordered one and given her red leather jacket so they can measure it. In the distance we heard children probably at school, horns and the whistling and squawking of geese and other birds. A simple meal of rice, vegetables and dahl, cooked was served to us on the houseboat.

2ⁿᵈ May

It had stopped raining so we took a shikara to the land and walked to the poste restante at the main post office. There was letter from my friend Stan, back in Norwich, short with no mention of money.

The two Australians, Brad and Kelly, who were staying on our houseboat were both sick, which made me wonder abut the hygiene here, or lack of it. Although the water looked clean here, we were downstream from many other houseboats. Down by the bridge where the poorer families live on far less luxurious boats, it was stinking. And it seemed like the toilet empties direct into the lake, where they also seemed to wash dishes and clothes.

3rd May

After breakfast we went on a shikara ride around Dahl lake. We were able to stretch out and relax on a mattress with cushions under a canopy. Very relaxing.

The view of the mountains was beautiful and tranquil. Nehru Park was in the middle of the lake, then Rup Lank (gold island)

with its four chiner trees. The houseboats were less crowded here. The view was even better with the reflections in the clear waters.   We could hear the sound of chanting and musical instruments from the shore.

Nighat Gardens were between the lake and the mountains. We decide to pay them a visit. They had been there since 1833, splendid gardens of grass, flowers and trees, with its own canal and cascades running down the middle and a series of terraces takes one up to the fine lake views.

To our left we saw Hari Parbat Fort on top of Sharika Hill. It was built 1592 to 1598, during the reign of Akbar. Visits were only possible with written permission from the Director of Tourism. Outside was a shrine to the 6th Sikh Guru.

On our way back, we passed the Hazratbal Mosque. New and shining white, supposed to house hair from the Prophet.

When we got back to the New Wild Rose, I read in a book that a trip on Dahl Lake was a sybaritic experience. None of us actually knew the word but we instinctively knew what it meant - fond of sensuous luxury or pleasure; self-indulgent.

4th May

A warm day, much spent just enjoying the sun on the houseboat.. Lesley, Brad and Kerry were all feeling better. Now I was slowing down! I felt fine.

We called in to see Yussef Baktoo in his office. He said that in Kashmir Lesley was "Puxley" and Alun was "Ali".

The guy who met us from the bus, Gulab Khar, told us a tale. When he was a baby of four years old, a vulture swept down and carried him off; his father quickly threw a stone and it hit the bird which dropped little Gulab ten feet and the father caught him. Lucky Gulab!

5th May

We spent most of the day lazing around on the deck of the houseboat, watching the clouds and shikara boats. We had a splendid view of snow-capped mountains. I bought a silver box, also earrings with coral.

The local Islamic people were fasting that day.

It rained heavily during the night.

6th May

Suddenly at 7 Am we were awoken by loud voices and knocking on the door.

"Quick, quick, come quick, water is coming into boat".

So with pounding heart I jumped out of bed and put on some clothes, making sure Lesley was doing the same. I am not sure she believed what was happening.

We rushed outside then Bashir says "No, it is OK, go to sleep, as they are bailing out the water with buckets."

Apparently one end of the boat was lower in the water and caused a panic.

By noon it was too hot to sit on the sun deck.

It was either a holiday or a strike.

7th May

Trying to find the Thomas Cook office was not easy despite the offers of help from the holiday company. Mr Kahr said it was at the Oberai Hotel.

Lesley bought some medicine called Amelast that contains dioxamide and tridazole, an intestinal anti-parasitic drug.

In the afternoon we went on a shikara ride to the beautiful lake Nageen to see the new Butterfly Houseboat, which looked palatial with beautiful paintings in the Mogul and Indian rooms, carvings in the Kashmir room, and in the Shikara room a bed shaped like a shikara.

On the way back we called at a carpet shop. I bought a woollen carpet on my previous visit to Kashmir in 1981 for £200, so did not want one this time, but Lesley bought a beautiful silk one for a deposit and then monthly payments when back in the UK. They will send it to her by air mail. Of course there will be duty on it so it will cost her over £400.

8th May

So far we had seen shikaras selling jewellery, now it was saffron. It's cheap though.

Lesley had developed a habit of saying "Maybe later" and inevitably they come back.

I wrote a letter to the Sitar shop to arrange a later date to meet the guy back in Delhi with the Sitar I bought as we would be there later than expected. I gave it to Jimmy to post.

9th May: The Valley of the Shepherds

We went by taxi to Pahalgam and a few miles more to the toll gate. It was raining hard. By the time we walked to Aru we were soaked.

The previous year we had camped by the river but now it was too wet so we are staying in the Rest House in the little town of Aru, before we start our pony trekking tomorrow. Our guide was another Ali.

The village lies on the left bank of the Aru river, which was a tributary of the Lidder river.

The village was a base camp for trekkers to the Kolahoi Glacier, the Tarsar-Marsar lakes and the Katrinag valley. It was also a base for the treks to Lidderwat, the Vishan-Kishansar lakes and Kangan.

Aru was situated at 9,000 feet. The population was less than 50.

10th May

We set off walking and sometimes on the ponies. The rain had eased off and the scenery was absolutely incredible. We walked for about two hours and when we got there, a place with no name, the tents were already pitched.

With the snow capped mountains and rushing stream, it was lovely. It rained again in the afternoon after we were served omelette and chips, but the tent with fly sheet and ground sheet was quite adequate.

11th May

We walked and rode towards Kolahai, crossing the snow line. Kolahoi Peak was the highest mountain in Kashmir with a peak elevation of 17,799 feet. Obviously we had no intention of going to the top!

But, as was typical here, they did not tell us what was happening and suddenly we were walking into the snow, with the ponies behind us along with my rucksack and shades which I would certainly need to avoid snow blindness at that height. "Ponies wait for us to come back," said Ali, "they not like snow."

159

So we stopped a little way past some empty huts. Ali and Martin, the Canadian guy that had joined us, were to walk on to see the glacier. We would go back. Fine with us.

The air was so thin that even cigarettes went out when one stopped puffing on them.

They returned after two hours. Martin was almost blind. The snow had become too deep and dangerous for them to continue. Ali should have known that. We are not mountaineers, were not equipped for that. This was supposed to be a pony trek.

So we returned to our camp, which we are told was called Lidderwatt, such a beautiful tranquil spot. Ali told us tales of who died here last year. Two fell off ponies crossing the river and one whilst rafting.

At some point we met an old chap that asked if we had any aspirins because his wife had toothache and he was on his way to walk to Pahalgam to buy some. He was barefooted. I had some in my bag and gave them to him. He gave me a small piece of nice black hash. Hash is no good for toothache.

On the way down, we stopped at a small shack. There was a smiling woman there with what may have been her daughter. She invited us to drink some chai. It was pink milky and salty, just what we needed. The girl was fascinated with Lesley and her hair.

As we moved along a track with low branches handing down that I had to duck under, my pony fell behind the others. As they disappeared behind some trees on bend, my pony panicked and started moving faster than it ever had before with me on its back. But as soon as it caught sight of the others, it slowed down again.

14th May

Back in Srinagar. Lazing about, floating about the lakes, getting high.

15th May

Another warm day. We tried go to pick up sweaters that we ordered but there was fighting in town so we couldn't go. Lesley had decided she did not want animal fur and ended up losing her red leather jacket as they had not returned it.

We were trying to get the "Numero Uno" hash that Ali spoke of. He reckoned that we had was 50% cow shit, even though we found it strong. In the evening we visited the other brother,

Jimmy, at his request, on a houseboat, called Jupiter. It was a bit boring; he just left after half an hour. Then it took us an hour to get a shikara home to the New Wild Rose.

Meanwhile I found the letter to the Sitar company that I gave to Jimmy to post, in the drawer in the living room. When I told him, he just said "no problem". Well not for you Jimmy, but I would not get my sitar now.

16th May: Sonamarg

163

That day we took a taxi to Sonamarg or Sonmarg. Beautiful mountain peaks with snow all around. We walked off towards the glacier but after a while we just stopped. It was so beautiful.

Lesley bought a musk ball; it's a lovely smell but a deer's testicle!

17th May

There was a curfew on in town that day due to a visit from some politician. Lesley had an upset stomach and cramps so we stayed on the boat; a massage with mustard oil helped.

Jimmy popped in and promised Numero Uno tomorrow and I gave him some cash. It was hard to get a good signal on the radio and the tape machine didn't work properly so there was not a lot of music, which was a shame.

18th May

We had planned go to Gulmarg but had put it off until the next day.

19th May

The taxi to Gulmarg did not turn up.

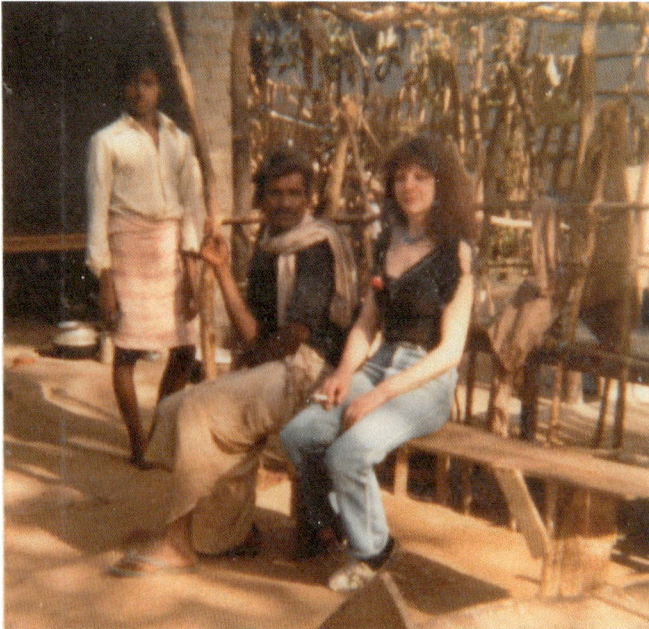

Instead we went to a shop, by Shikara, that was selling some beautiful carved walnut items. I bought some carved candlesticks, some statuettes including a dancing Buddha, a sewing box and several carved cigarette boxes that they would ship back to the UK. They also had a beautiful carved dining table with six matching chairs but that was out of my price range. The cigarette box was a novelty; one put about ten cigarettes in the lower compartment, then when one lifted and dropped the top section, one appeared on the grove in the lid.

20th May

We wasted much of the afternoon trying to get to Thomas Cook's, which turned out to be at Johanson Travel not the Grindleys Hotel as we had been told that money was coming.

This was after being told for ten days that money for us was at Grindleys. But there was still no money there. So we sent a message to Thomas Cooks in Delhi to tell them to keep the money there.

Jimmy, who did not turn up last night where we were supposed to meet him at the Tourist Office and waited, came to see us and said he had been waiting for us on Houseboat Jupiter. He said that he would bring the smoke to the New Wild Rose tonight.

We never did get Numero Uno from Jimmy but I did get my money back.

I had asked for tickets back to Delhi tomorrow, but so far there are none, so we will be here another day. I had arranged to pay our bill later, either in Delhi or back in the UK. They said that was no problem. Yeah, like my sitar!

I just wanted to get back to Delhi, pick up some money and confirm the flight home. If we needed to wait a week, we could go to Kulu and Manali and get stoned, I thought.

The people here were all friendly enough, but they never say they don't know and brush everything aside as if nothing mattered to them but of course it did. In fact everything mattered. There was a lot of ignorance and lack of experience. Many lived such limited lives. They didn't understand tourists and travellers, think we are all super rich; well compared to so many we are, after all, we are there on holiday often living like kings, miles from our home, and they had so little and life can be hard. They don't even realise the harm that can come from washing in the sewage of Dahl lake; they don't know that it was getting worse because they are polluting it themselves.

Many people are fighting for freedom, freedom from India. They mistakenly, in my opinion, think they would be batter off as part of Pakistan because they are Moslem. It's not violent in Kashmir, completely different to Pakistan. They are too bound by superficial religious appearance and ritual.

The family structure was very strong but men could take multiple wives and, strangely enough, although they would all smoke hash with us, they hid it away from each other; and many were secret alcohol drinkers.

They often used smiles and pleasant offers of chai or small gifts to buy their way into our pockets.

But still, Kashmir was one of the safest and most beautiful parts of the world.

21st May

Suddenly Yussef told us our money was at Grindleys, so off went go again. But of course it's not. "The money has not been sent", they told us.

Then suddenly our flight back to Heathrow was confirmed for the 25th, four days time, so we planned to get the bus back to Delhi tomorrow.

In some ways I thought I'll be glad to be back in Norwich. In other ways I felt I could travel on.

22nd May: Delhi and Homeward Bound

The bus ride back to Delhi was almost 24 hours, but it's the best one yet, with no problems. We spend some time in the driver's cabin, up front, so some fantastic views.

23rd May

Back in Delhi at 7 AM at the Ringo Guest House with air conditioning and shower, opposite the Indian Oil Building.

We went to Thomas Cooks and picked up some money. It's been there all the time.

We bought some cheap chokers and beaded necklaces and some very cheap women's shirts from the underground market where they had a sale. Some were less than £1 each and I know I can sell them for at least £6 each.

Ali met us and had Lesley's lost jeans from Rajasthan. He took her to a night club in the evening. When they got back to the hotel, he was clearly a little drunk.

24th May.

I went back to the market and bought more cotton blouses, now my rucksack was packed very full. It was far too hot and uncomfortable outside during the day.

In the evening we went to the Mandarin room at the Hotel Imperial.

Then we went to see Ali and on to the airport.

25th May

We arrived back in the UK at Heathrow Airport.

I walked through customs without a problem.

Lesley got pulled by the customs team. They found her little musk ball and, she told me later, she said "That's not what you think it is."

So they did a strip search and called in a doctor and she had to hand over her little stash from her personal space and was busted. Fat Stan had come to pick us up with another guy called Nigel and we were waiting in the arrivals hall for Lesley when there was an announcement for Stan. Nigel went in to learn that Lesley was being detained for a few hours and so he gave her enough money to get back to Norwich by bus or train, as we could not wait.

A couple of months later, we took her to Uxbridge Court where she as fined £100. Everyone else in court while we were there had suitcases full of drugs.

AFTERTHOUGHTS

I had made three trips to India. The first, pretty much out of the blue because when we left the UK we had intended to travel only as far a Turkey, in a van. There were four of us. None of us had very much money. I had left UK with just about £60, three weeks wages in those days. By the time we reached Antalya, in Turkey on the southern coast, I had just £20 left. We slept either in the van or in a tent until we reached Istanbul, where we rented cheap rooms. After that, we slept in Turkey in the open. From Turkey, Keith and I took a boat eastwards, intending to travel to Beirut then back to Istanbul to meet up again with the others. On the boat, however, we were advised not to go to Beirut, so instead hitch-hiked across Syria into Iraq and on the Baghdad, then on by bus to Tehran. Then we headed east across Iran, Afghanistan, Pakistan and into India. The main problem for me was lack of money, so not being able to eat the food I should have been eating and staying in cheap and often dirty hotels. I ran out of money in Kabul, a dirty city but cheap and friendly. I sold a few items such as shirts and a compass and met a wealthy German guy called Helmutt, who helped us get to India, by plane from Lahore to Amritsar, one of the first passenger planes after the end of the Pakistan-India war. In Amritsar, we stayed for free at The golden Temple and I hitched a truck ride to Delhi.

I struggled on very little money, receiving just a few pounds in mail from the UK. Keith went on alone to Nepal. I became ill and spend a week in hospital (free) in Delhi, suffering from dysentery and hepatitis. I tried to travel back overland to the UK but became ill again and again, being hospitalised in Kabul and Tehran, from where I had to take a flight back to London, which my parents paid for. I was 22-years-old. Looking back, it's easy to say I should have had more sense.

Yet looking back, it was also a pretty dumb thing to do, although very educational and an experience that I valued. But it was hard work in the east, with such different people, customs, lifestyles, religions, languages, foodstuff, politics and the divisions of wealth and poverty.

That was a disastrous trip, not only did I and Keith became ill, but after we left Turkey my good friend John Sullivan was killed when the van crashed in Antalya; the other passenger, Mike, was seriously hurt, broken leg, broken ribs and bang on the head. I did not even find out what had happened until I was back in Kabul, months later, and by chance met somebody that I knew from Norwich, Pete Roscoe, who was on his way to India.

From the moment we had left the UK, everywhere we went, we managed to buy hash, in every country we passed through with the exceptions of Iraq and Iran. In Iran, we actually stayed on an opium farm run by a licensed farmer who also supplied it illegally. He was also the village policeman.

That tail is told in my book "All About My Hat The Hippy Trail, 1972"

What did I learn?

The variety of people in our world.

The generosity and care we received from people with so little.

That I had people that I could call on to help when all else failed.

To travel with enough money to get one through and get one home safely.

To take more care of health regarding hygiene and diet.

So my next trips to India, both by plane, recorded in this book, were 1981 and 1985.

By this time many places had already changed in respect of politics and freedom, and it was not so possible to travel overland.

1981 was a two week holiday. 1985 was a two month journey.

At both times I had more money, enough as I thought, being older and wiser, as I thought. Yet in both cases we spent our money faster than we had anticipated and had to write home for more.

Of course another problem that was easy to have forgotten, was that contact with family and friends back in the UK was not instant and easy. A phone call had to be booked a week in advance and one had to hope that the call would be answered. Otherwise, it meant booking another call. Also in those days not everyone in the UK had a phone in their house and nobody had a mobile (cell) phone.

We were lucky to have booked the holidays through travel companies that were able to help us out.

So I'd reiterate my advice, make sure one has enough funds and remember, cash and bankers cards can be lost or stolen (as can possessions and passports).

Delhi and Agra, had changed noticeably since 1972 since I had visited those cities.

They were more populated with more traffic, more noise, more dirt and more beggars and hasslers on the streets. Also more "richer" tourists. Kashmir was attracting people with money, staying on houseboats, often isolated and even protected from the people and poverty on the streets. Corruption, baksheesh, favouritism and bureaucracy were all more common – you will have read about our problems getting seated on planes that had been overbooked.

One of the favourite sayings of many people was "no problem". Either they did not see a problem, did not see it as important or simply did not care. Yet paying baksheesh in advance would often avoid those problems.

'Jimmy', on the houseboat in Kashmir in 1985 never did post the letter that he had promised to post; that cost me a sitar.

Many Indians won't say that they don't know; instead they tell one what they think. An example was when we were told that our funds were at a bank when they were not and had not even been sent.

I certainly would not advise anyone to drive a vehicle in India. The rule of the road everywhere was "Might is Right". Walkers and people with carts pulled by animals got out of the way of cars, which got out of the way of buses, which got out of the way of trucks. Everyone was listening out for the loudest horns approaching them. Everyone in the cities seemed to drive using their horns more than indicators. Of course walkers and those with animal-pulled carts had no horns.

At one point in this book, you will see a photo taken from a rickshaw on a road in Delhi; you can see pedestrians, bicycles, rickshaws, cars, buses, trucks and even an elephant.

Of course food is another problem: you may have heard of "Delhi belly".

The difference between western and India food and water, the way in which so much ghee is used, often the lack of hygiene, that does not cause serious problems for locals, almost inevitably causes some problems for westerners on short holidays. Often these problems are short-lived, being simply a matter of adjusting, but one does not want or need to spend a few days feeling ill especially on a short trip.

At all times, one needs to be aware of thieves and conmen on the streets. People, both men and women, that will simply want to take advantage of you.

There are those that will simply try to pick your pocket or steal your bag; there are those that ask for money and won't take no for an answer; there are those that will tell lies and try to mislead you for their own advantage; there are those that say they just want to practice their English and end up taking you to a shop where actually they are friendly and often the craftsmanship is fine. That tactic includes foreigners as well as locals.

Thankfully those people, the ones that want to get you to but something, are in the minority and, in my opinion, far better than thieves. People without jobs or sponsors have to make their money. Beg, steal or sell their wares. Of course, in the cities, like most big cities, there are also drug dealers about on the streets and many of whom are also dishonest or unscrupulous, selling anything from hard drugs to fake drugs.. The majority will be friendly and helpful or simply stand and stare. One certainly has to become used to people staring. Also some people don't want their photographs taken and will ask for money or become very angry, whilst others will ask you to take a photograph of them with or without you.

The gap between wealth and poverty is sometimes atrocious and sickening. One can do nothing about it. In Delhi we made a quick visit to a five star hotel. Inside was spotless and elegant and a cup of tea cost about £5. Right outside the guarded gates that led to the garden from the street, was a tiny chai stall where a cup cost pennies and the street was littered with rubbish and rubble. One sees street food stalls selling hot and cold dished whilst donkey-pulled carts trundle by in the dust, dropping their crap as they go. Many people are unaware of hygiene or unable to do anything about it. Certainly it is essential to ensure that even bottled water in restaurants is actually bottled water and not just from the tap, or to use purification tablets.

But all that is India. That is part of the experience. But just as it is wise to wear a safety helmet on a building site anywhere, one needs to take care and precautions..

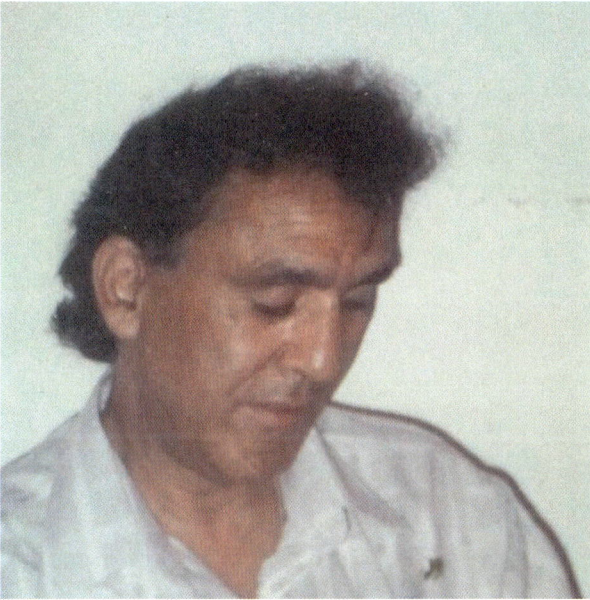

ALI BAKTOO

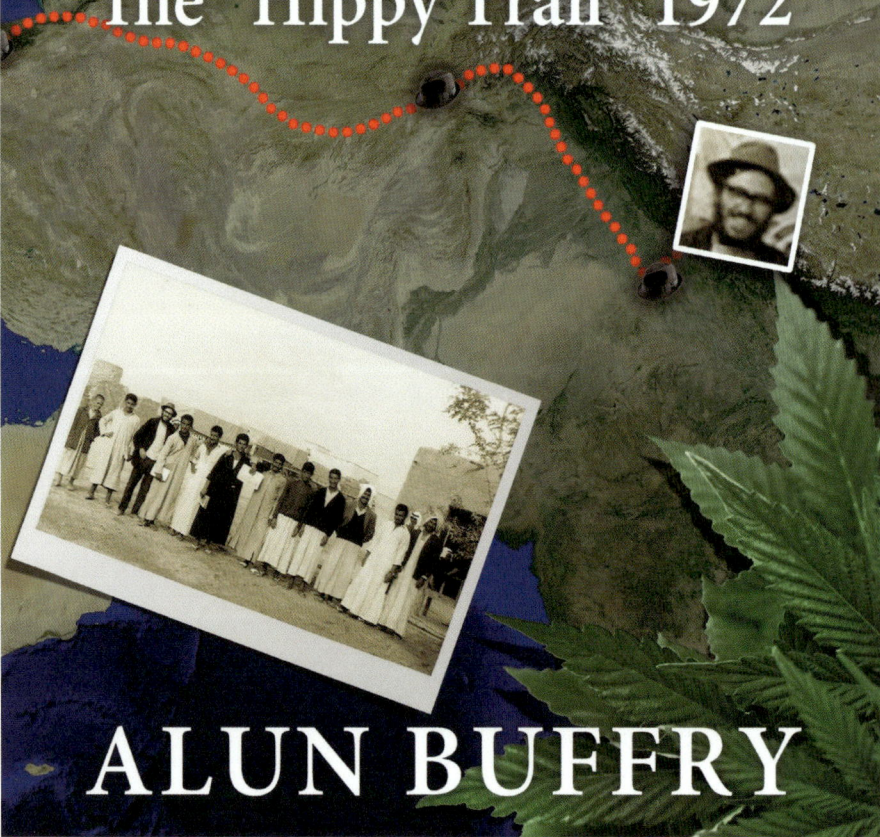

All About
My Hat
The "Hippy Trail" 1972

ALUN BUFFRY

MYHAT
IN EGYPT
Through the Eyes of a God

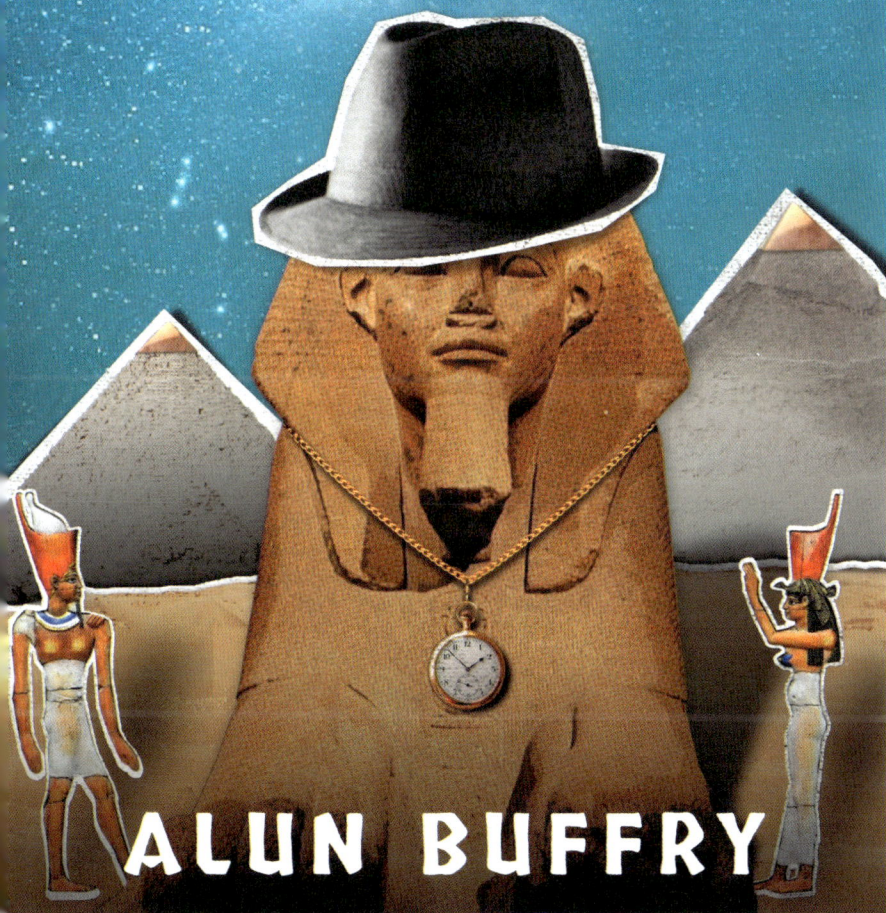

ALUN BUFFRY

TIME FOR CANNABIS

The Prison Years
1991 to 1995

Alun Buffry

ALUN BUFFRY

THE EFFIE ENIGMA

THE MOTHERLESS MOTHERS

Alun Buffry

IF ONLY SUOMI

My Life of Joy

Alun Buffry

And There I Was

Alun Buffry

INSIDE MY HAT
AND
OTHER HEADS

ALUN BUFFRY · JACQUI MALKIN · WINSTON MATTHEWS
SARAH DOUGAN AKA SARAH SATIVA · PHIL MONK
ROCKY VAN DE BENDERSKUM · STEVE COOK
MELISSA DOORDAUGHTER AKA ARIADNE SNAIL

Words of Weed and Wisdom

Alun Buffry , Clara O'Donnell, Jacqui Malkin,
Jezza Austin, Mars Bilters, Melissa Doordaughter,
Phil Monk, Rocky van de Benderskum, Ryan Kief,
Sarah Dougan and Steve Cook

LEGALISE
and
UTILISE

COMMEMORATIVE
EDITION
2021

Printed in Great Britain
by Amazon